DISCIPLINING FOUCAULT

Thinking Gender
Edited by Linda J. Nicholson

Also published in the series

DISCIPLINING FOUCAULT

FEMINISM, POWER, AND THE BODY

JANA SAWICKI

Routledge   New York   London

Published in 1991 by

Routledge
An imprint of Routledge, Chapman and Hall, Inc.
29 West 35 Street
New York, NY 10001

Published in Great Britain by

Routledge
11 New Fetter Lane
London EC4P 4EE

Library of Congress Cataloging in Publication Data

Sawicki, Jana.
    Disciplining Foucault : feminism, power, and the body / Jana Sawicki.
      p. cm.
    Includes bibliographical references and index.
    ISBN 0-415-90187-1 (hard).—ISBN 0-415-90188-X (pbk.)
    1. Feminist theory. 2. Foucault, Michel. I. Title.
HQ1190.C67   1991
305.42'01—dc20   72447   91-142
                                  CIP

British Library cataloguing in publication data also available.

To Laurie and Ouli

Contents

Acknowledgments

Many individuals, organizations and institutions provided the support and encouragement necessary to complete this collection of essays. I am happy to have the opportunity to acknowledge them here.

Although all of the essays collected here were written after I left graduate school, work done on my dissertation served as their foundation. I am indebted to Robert D. Cumming, David Hoy and Charles Larmore for supporting that project.

I am grateful to the Women in the Curriculum Project at the University of Maine for providing financial support in the form of two summer grants that enabled me to begin research on feminist theory in the early eighties. Mary Childers and Deborah Pearlman were especially important resources to me as friends and experts in Women's Studies at a time when I was just getting my feet wet. I also owe thanks to the University of Maine for granting me a Summer Faculty Research Award in the summer of 1987 that made it possible for me to travel to Paris and to Boston where I did research for Chapter 4. The Women's Studies Program at the Massachusetts Institute of Technology generously provided office space and institutional affiliation as a Visiting Scholar during my sabbatical in 1987–88. Many thanks go to Joni Seager, Director of Women's Studies at MIT, for her assistance and support that year.

My colleagues in Philosophy at the University of Maine, Michael Howard, Doug Allen, Erling Skorpen, Ralph Hjelm and Jeff White, have also been incredibly supportive since my arrival in 1981. They have consistently encouraged me to pursue interdisciplinary work in Feminist Studies over the years. Not only have they encouraged me, but many of them have been pioneers in introducing feminist materials into their own curricula and research. This made being the lone woman in the Department for eight years a truly extraordinary experience. I owe special thanks to Mike Howard for comments and conversations at every stage of this project. Thanks are also owed to Jean Berger, our Department Administrative Associate, for the warmth, humor and patience she always exhibited when helping me with wordprocessing. Finally, I want to acknowledge the many students in Feminist Studies courses from whom I have learned how important it is to develop strategies for bridging differences.

Early drafts of several of the essays were presented at meetings of the Society for Women in Philosophy (Eastern Division), the Radical Philosophy Association and the Socialist Feminist Philosophers Association (SOFPHIA). These organizations are remarkably committed to providing a sympathetic atmosphere for developing philosophy as a form of social criticism. Part of that support includes constructive and critical engagement with the ideas being developed by their members. I am deeply grateful for their presence in the profession and their influence on my own development as a professional philosopher.

At the end of each chapter, I have already acknowledged many of the individuals who generously gave their time and energy to commenting on different papers in this collection or to discussing ideas contained in them. Nevertheless, I want to mention some of them again here. Iris Young, Sandra Bartky, Ann Ferguson, Linda Nicholson, and Nancy Fraser have provided encouragement, conversation and criticism when I needed it. I feel fortunate to have entered the profession after them. Thanks are also due to my editor, Maureen MacGrogan, for her confidence and patience. Finally, I must acknowledge my debt to Linda Singer whose renegade style, stimulating conversation and frequent words of support are deeply missed.

This project might still be on my desk if not for the encouragement and gentle prodding of those closest to me. I would like to thank Ada Harrigan, David DeKing and John Sickel for their love and friendship over the years. Laurie Benjamin provided the final push that enabled me to finish.

Note on the text

Chapter 1 first appeared in *Hypatia*, published by Indiana University Press.

Chapter 2 is reprinted from *Feminism and Foucault: Reflections on Resistance*, edited by Irene Diamond and Lee Quinby. Copyright © 1988 by Irene Diamond and Lee Quinby. Reprinted with the permission of Northeastern University Press.

Chapter 3 is reprinted from *After Foucault: Humanistic Knowledge, Post Modern Challenges*, edited by Jonathan Arac. Copyright © 1988 by Rutgers, the State University Press. Reprinted by permission of Rutgers University Press.

Introduction
Disciplining Foucault:
Personal Reflections

Each of my works is part of my own biography.[1]
—Michel Foucault

Most of the available theories of reading, writing, sexuality, or any other cultural production are built upon male narratives of gender . . . narratives which persistently tend to reproduce themselves in feminist theories.[2]
—Teresa de Lauretis

It is by now commonplace to point out that women are alienated from the discourses of Western culture, even the revolutionary ones. Recent French psychoanalytic theorists such as Luce Irigaray and Julia Kristeva both have suggested that Western cultural discourses are univocally masculinist. They claim that these so-called "phallocentric" discourses offer no place for women to speak except insofar as they speak in ways that men have preordained. Thus, women's only alternatives are to speak in a masculine voice, construct a new language, or be silent.

Michel Foucault offered a slightly more optimistic view of the relationship between language and power. He would have rejected the view that the power of phallocentric discourse is total. Instead, for Foucault, discourse is ambiguous and plurivocal. It is a site of conflict and contestation. Thus, women can adopt and adapt language to their own ends. They may not have total control over it but then neither do men. Choice, chance and power govern our relationships to the discourses we employ. And, to be sure, the choice to appropriate "male-stream" theoretical traditions involves risks that should be analyzed.

As a feminist in the academy I feel obligated to look for the evidence of power and privilege in my own theoretical and methodological commitments and predilections. Our attachments and outlooks are rooted in both individual and collective

1

histories. They reveal as much about our historical and cultural milieu as they do about us as individuals. Reflection upon the conditions governing individual choices is vital if we are to avoid unwitting capitulation to the very forces that we are resisting.

We must continually ask ourselves why we write. What do we hope to achieve through our writing? This is an especially important question for academic feminists since there are so many pressures to write without regard for audience or purpose, and to privilege our conversations with men and their traditions.

Deborah Cameron has written: "Men do not control meaning at all. Rather women elect to use modes of expression men can understand because that is the best way to get men to listen."[3] How many of the choices of feminists in the academy are influenced by the fact that surviving in them has meant getting powerful men to listen? For whom do we write as feminist intellectuals? Why do we chose one discourse over another?

Clearly, there is no single set of answers to these questions. But I would like to answer them for myself. I want to share a brief personal narrative about significant forces that shaped my early development as a philosopher and feminist, and hence, about some of the significant forces that shaped the production of the essays in this collection. My aim is to bring into relief the fundamental ambivalence that I have felt as a feminist philosopher, and some of the internal conflicts that were resolved in various ways by the choices that I made. This is not simply a brief chapter in my intellectual biography, a project of dubious value in itself, but rather a glimpse at the disciplinary practices that constitute women as intellectuals in the academy—practices that both enable and subjugate us. I suspect that my story is not unlike those of many others.

Of course, it is important to point out that many feminists did not enter the academy at all because they saw so little room in it for exploring feminist issues. As a graduate student I was very aware that Ti-Grace Atkinson, a former graduate student who had left my program before finishing (and before I arrived), had written an important early radical feminist book, *Amazon Odyssey*, in space provided to her by the Philosophy Department, while living "on the margins" of the institution. She continued to be a source of inspiration and of doubt about my choice to continue in the program. My own feminist consciousness emerged after I had made the choice to enter the male-dominated profession of philosophy. While I continue to have great respect for feminists who write as independent scholars, I also believe that there are important struggles for feminists within the university, not the least of which are those that have a direct impact on curriculum and pedagogy and hence on the many students who are often profoundly influenced by their experiences during their years as undergraduates. There are, of course, also struggles at the level of theory. If, as Teresa de Lauretis suggests, most theories available to feminists are based on "male narratives of gender," then considerable criticism, revision and reorientation of the traditions of male discourse is necessary. And insofar as we internalize these narratives, considerable self-criticism is required as well.

The telling of stories like mine has often been reserved for informal conversations among feminists struggling to define a sense of place in the academy without losing touch with feminism as a social movement. One place for such discussions has been the meetings and conferences of the Society for Women in Philosophy—an organization to which I owe most of whatever sense of comfort I have been able to achieve as a feminist philosopher. Indeed, I am most grateful to the pioneers in "feminist philosophy," a phrase that seemed oxymoronic when I was a graduate student. Writing about myself, even in an "Introduction" (the discursive space reserved for such forays into the non-philosophical), is difficult. On some level, I still regard the distant, disinterested and self-effacing style of most philosophical prose as appropriate even in a setting such as this. If we are to free ourselves from rigid adherence to the standards and practices of our disciplines that constrain and neutralize feminism, personal reflection on the conditions out of which our discourses are produced is crucial.

Who are the "authors" of my discourse on Foucault and feminist theory? What conditions governed what could be said, how it could be said and whether I could say it? What were the political implications of the choices that I made? What were the possibilities for resistance within the confines of my discipline?

Even today, women in the university are defined to a great extent by relationships to men—whether as students, research assistants, assistant professors, or "disciples." If a woman is never taken under wing by a benevolent male mentor, in order to survive, she must still become a disciple in a broader sense, that is, she must submit herself to the ideas and methods of the great men in her field. She is expected to take their questions seriously, adopt their languages, and master their ideas, even if only temporarily.

For me, this process was filled with conflict. The absence of women in the canon, let alone the philosophy classroom, the adversarial method of argument, and the dominance of the analytic method of philosophy that seemed to me at the time to be too narrow to be able to contribute much to substantive analyses of pressing social and political questions, all contributed to my doubts about philosophy.[4] At the same time, I experienced the sense of empowerment that comes from "mastering" a body of learning, developing analytical and critical skills, learning to argue effectively, and surviving in a male-dominated profession.

My interest in Foucault developed toward the end of my training in a graduate program focussed primarily on the analytic tradition of philosophy. A feminist at heart—albeit a neophyte to feminist theory—I had had little opportunity to integrate nascent feminist interests into my curriculum. Existentialism intrigued me because it was one of the few philosophies that addressed the sensual, emotional, embodied and experiential origins of theory. At least the existentialists believed that philosophy should make a difference in how one lived one's life. Moreover, Nietzsche, Kierkegaard and Sartre gave philosophical legitimacy to inquiries into sexuality, desire and power—all inquiries that I regarded as central to my own life and to feminism.

Realizing that my tastes in philosophy were marginal to those of most of my professors, I found ways to pursue what I now regard as feminist interests in non-feminist ways. I read Nietzsche's genealogy of power and slave morality and struggled unsuccessfully to find redeeming features of his passages on women and Jews. I read Hegel on Antigone, philosophical debates about pornography and censorship, Heidegger's critique of technology and Merleau-Ponty on the lived body—while also qualifying in major areas of twentieth century analytic philosophy. Sensitive to the negative stereotypes about continental philosophy that flourished in my program, I still felt compelled by it.

My choice to write a dissertation on Foucault represented an act of rebellion and accommodation. As I began to pursue the topic, one of my advisors strongly urged me to write a dissertation on Sartre instead. He pointed out that Sartre addressed more traditional philosophical problems. And after all, he seemed to imply, de Beauvoir was a feminist. But I did not think that the philosophical world needed another Sartre dissertation. Like Nietzsche, Foucault was a writer whose philosophical status was questionable. He was a bit outrageous. He did not produce arguments; he wrote histories. He was not developing a theory of truth or rationality, but rather analyzing the relations of power and knowledge that underpin certain understandings of truth and rationality. Unlike Nietzsche, he was explicitly political. One of his principal aims was to restore the socio-critical dimension to philosophy. No doubt, Foucault appealed to me partly because he gave voice to some of my own doubts about philosophy, to my sense that there was something constraining and arbitrary about the boundaries and the dominant methods of the discipline. Even more important for me was that fact that Foucault made issues of sexual liberation central to his research and political interventions.

How was this an act of accommodation? Despite Foucault's unpopularity in my own graduate program, he was becoming curiously legitimate. Certainly more legitimate than any feminist topic would have been. Another of my advisors, a relatively marginal but still powerful figure in the Department, had steered me in this direction. Moreover, established philosophers like Richard Rorty and Ian Hacking were taking Foucault seriously.

Then, of course, there was the fact that I would be asked to subject Foucault's ideas to rigorous philosophical scrutiny. I would make him philosophically relevant by rationally reconstructing his critique of humanism and power.

Thus, I began a four year writing project. Before finishing, I was hired as the first woman in a relatively progressive philosophy department. Ironically, my background in French poststructuralism became an asset. In this surprisingly supportive context, I began to develop and extend Foucault's insights about power, identity and sexuality through an analysis of issues in American feminism. Feminism became increasingly central to my research, but remained marginal to the dissertation. (The word "feminism" appeared in the Preface.) After finishing my dissertation, I received funding twice from the Women in the Curriculum project at the University of Maine in order to develop my background in feminist theory and introduce the material into the classroom. Both the University Faculty Research Grant Program and the Women's Development Program generously supported ongoing research and writing projects. Nevertheless, I remember a distinct feeling of anxiety concerning my position at this time. I felt pressure to defend my interest in Foucault to many feminists. At the same time I was aware that the fact that my discourse appealed to Foucault, that I had become a Foucault "expert," was its redeeming feature from the perspective of men in positions of power over me.

Now, over three years after tenure, I am in a better position to reflect on the power relations out of which my philosophical work has emerged. Assessing the political implications of this work requires sensitivity to the changing contexts and audiences in which it developed. Whereas writing about Foucault in graduate school represented an act of resistance to the hegemony of more conservative and "apolitical" trends in philosophy, my choice to use Foucault for feminist analysis was less obviously resistant. It did not need to be, for I was being encouraged to develop the work. More importantly, it was becoming increasingly legitimate to write about Foucault. Indeed, a veritable Foucault industry has sprung up over the past decade. Nonfeminist critical theories, and, to a lesser extent, the feminists who appropriate them, have become commodities. Foucault's discourse has become authoritative despite his own efforts to efface his authority. Appeals to this authority have lent credibility to feminist scholarship in some quarters that it might not otherwise have had. In addition, Women's Studies publications also flourished during the eighties.

In many respects, my work flowed with these trends rather than against them. Insofar as I found the trends to be progressive, I had no reason not to be a part of them. But there is also something unsettling in the rise of poststructuralism, and more recently, postmodernism in the American academy. The increased vulnerability of Women's Studies programs as we face the possibility of severe economic recession is even more distressing. We have reached a point where it is important to ask whether poststructuralism itself is in danger of becoming as normalizing as the discourses that it criticizes.

What does one do with this discomfort? First and foremost one must acknowledge it and live with it. My own discomfort bolsters self-critical impulses that keep me asking the kinds of questions being raised here. Secondly, discomfort can become an occasion for resisting efforts to domesticate poststructuralism, that is, to neutralize its radical and subversive elements. Third, and this is related to the problems associated with the domestication or assimilation of poststructuralism within the American academy, one must resist those appropriations of poststructuralism which subtly undermine gender, race and class based critical theories.

As the following essays make clear, Foucault's poststructuralism does not entail a complete rejection of identity based politics, but rather the search for a true identity as a basis for universal emancipation. One's commitment to poststructuralist methods and analysis must itself always be subject to reappraisal. In other words, a fourth response to the discomfort that arises as these discourses become increasingly legitimate must be an openness to discarding or moving beyond them insofar as they become constraining, disabling, or compromising. One of the redeeming features of Foucault's discourse for me has been its continual resistance to efforts to turn it into a political orthodoxy. Foucault's discourse invites its own critique. Moreover, the shifts in the trajectory of his research were evidence of his willingness to surpass himself.

Defined in retrospect, the overall project of these essays has been to lay out the basic features of a Foucauldian feminism that is compatible with feminism as a pluralistic and *emancipatory* radical politics. My reading of Foucault emphasizes the later works in which power and subjectivity are at the center of his analysis. I also attempt to flesh out Foucault's undeveloped remarks about resistance and struggle in an effort to show how his discourse can be used to support specific liberatory political struggles, namely, struggles for sexual and reproductive freedom. At the same time, I offer what I hope will be taken as constructive critiques of certain tendencies in current feminist analyses that suppress differences among women and thereby overlook the differential impact on women of classism, racism, heterosexism and so forth. In the final analysis, these essays might be read as an effort to develop a radically pluralist feminism. It has been suggested that pluralist political strategies may be conservative in the United States context where pluralism is a dominant value, and that stressing differences within feminism can only fragment oppositional movements and enhance the increasingly concentrated power of global patriarchal capitalism.

The radical pluralism that I envision is distinct from liberal pluralism in the following ways. First, it operates with a relational and dynamic model of identity as constantly in formation in a hierarchal context of power relations at the microlevel of society. It recognizes plurality both within and between subjects. Thus, it departs from liberal pluralism which represents political power as dispersed and decentralized among competing interest groups that have a relatively stable identity and compete on an equal basis for political influence and representation.

Second, radical pluralism operates with an expanded sense of the political. It politicizes social and personal relationships usually overlooked within liberal theory. Indeed, radical pluralism politicizes theory as well. It treats theories as practices that serve as instruments of domination as well as liberation. At the same time, it involves building theories. But in so doing it adopts historically inflected categories and attends to the theoretical prerequisites for addressing diversity. Thus, it may uncover experiences of domination often overlooked within traditional emancipatory theories. One could argue that a political strategy that is attentive to differences, to using and bridging them, is vital if we are to build the global networks of resistance necessary for resisting global forms of domination.

Finally, radical pluralism is distinct from liberalism insofar as it challenges hegemonic power structures. It is based on a form of incrementalism in which the distinction between reform and revolution is collapsed. Yet, this is not an incrementalism based on a narrow definition of politics, nor is it one that denies the need for major structural transformation, or the existence of hegemonies based on class, race, gender and other forms of domination. It is an incrementalism that recognizes domination, but also represents the social field as a dynamic, multidimensional set of relationships containing possibilities for liberation as well as domination. In developing the outlines of a radically pluralist feminism, I have found Foucault's discourse to be immensely useful.

My earliest essay, "Foucault and Feminism: Towards a Politics of Difference," was my first attempt to integrate previous work on Foucault with feminist theory. It was written at a time when feminists of color were again challenging dominant feminist theories and organizations for failing to address their issues and experiences. White, middle-class feminism had unwittingly embraced universal categories and concepts that erased or occluded differences among women. The political critique of feminist theory that originated among black, poor and third-world women gave a flesh and blood significance to poststructuralist accounts of the suppression of difference in the constitution of identity that was much more compelling than any philosophical arguments could ever produce. I seized upon the idea of a "politics" as opposed to a "philosophy" of difference in order to emphasize the fact that theoretical practices are also practices of power that can perpetuate domination insofar as they overlook or ignore certain struggles. I argued that Foucault's genealogical critiques of the inhibiting and dominating effects of "total" theories such as liberalism and Marxism were useful in developing a radical alternative to these traditional revolutionary theories—an alternative that, in its appreciation of the heterogeneity, complexity and discontinuity of power relations, was more successful than prevailing theories had been in accounting for the role of new social movements (for instance, the women's movement, the gay and lesbian liberation movement, the ecology movement, the civil rights movement, the peace movement, and so forth) in a radical politics. In appropriating Foucault for feminism, I amplified his suggestive remarks about resistance and struggle both within and between subjects to account for the struggles over differences going on within feminism. I also valued his analytic of power because it supported feminists' insights about the need to analyze the politics of personal relations and everyday life, and accounted for our participation in reproducing systems of domination despite our conscious protests against specific forms of it. Foucault described how power grips us at the point where our desires and our very sense of the possibilities for self-definition are constituted.

Finally, I was intrigued by Foucault's ability to establish a position within the contradictions and tensions that plague any efforts to develop an emancipatory theory and politics in the modern world without feeling compelled to resolve them. In other words, his philosophy embraced the theoretical tensions that result when one acknowledges that we are both victims and agents within systems of domination, that our discourses can extend relations of domination at the same time that they are critical of them, and that any emancipatory theory bears the traces of its origins in specific historical relations of power/knowledge.

In retrospect, I think that I overlooked the gaps in Foucault's critical philosophy—his inattention to the macro-structures of power and his lack of normative clarity—because I found his critique of past efforts to establish total theories, and to provide absolute foundations for them, to be compelling. Moreover, I believed that Foucault's project was compatible with efforts to develop emancipatory theories that addressed the macrostructures of power and appealed to values such as justice, liberty and human dignity. Foucault was not providing an alternative theory, a point about which I was not entirely clear in this first essay, but rather a way of looking at our theories of self and society and a method for re-evaluating them, for freeing up possibilities for new forms of experience that might lead to a different understanding of theory, of ourselves, of reality.

The second essay, "Identity Politics and Sexual Freedom," followed immediately from the first and expands its discussion of feminism and sexual liberation. Part of my original attraction to Foucault's discourse was its attention to the question of sexual liberation. Foucault and feminists both challenged the sexual liberationism of the sixties for related reasons. Both recognized that power relations governing sexuality run deeper than is presupposed by strategies that simply aim to lift restrictions on sexual behavior. At the same time, Foucault would have been critical of feminist approaches that appealed to an essential and liberatory feminine desire repressed within patriarchal society. He had already criticized the essentialism in the homosexual liberation movement for its failure to get beyond the notion of a fixed sexual identity and its consequent participation in modern disciplinary technologies of sex. I was struck by the overlap between Foucault's problematization of sexual liberationist strategies and feminist debates concerning sexuality and power sparked by disagreements over questions concerning pornography and lesbian sadomasochism. I used Foucault's critique of the repressive hypothesis in order to illuminate similarities in the positions of opposing camps in the so-called feminist "sex wars" and to point beyond existing alternatives. At the same time, I used the essay to flesh out the practical implications of Foucault's critique of essentialist categories.

Foucault's reluctance to make political recommendations had always bothered me despite the fact that I understood some of his reasons for it. Feminist movements must develop political strategies. Thus, I endorsed efforts to build political movements that are sensitive to the dangers of authoritarianism, ethnocentrism and political vanguardism. Women of color in the U.S. certainly recognized the importance of coalition politics as a way of building bridges between women and men engaged in struggles against domination. Coalition building rooted in an appreciation of certain commonalities in our struggles combined with a form of consciousness raising that aimed to highlight the limits of our individual experiences, rather than to point to shared experiences, appeared to me to be a viable strategy for building a more inclusive, pluralistic feminist politics. Although there is now an increased sensitivity to differences among women in academic feminism, we have only scratched the surface of the barriers that prevent feminism from becoming radically pluralistic. In the meantime, I still agree with Gayle Rubin, whom I endorsed in this essay, that it is a mistake to view feminism as capable of providing a total account of domination and oppression.

"Feminism and the Power of Foucauldian Discourse" was an invited paper written for a collection of essays designed to chart the impact of Foucault on humanistic studies, for better or worse. I was asked to respond to an essay by Isaac Balbus, a male feminist defending Chodorow's mothering theory against Foucault's alleged attack on the possibility of developing a true and emancipatory discourse. In his essay, Balbus argued that Foucault's discourse "disciplines" feminism insofar as it imposes constraints upon it that threaten to undermine the project of a feminist transformation of society. The role reversals in this pair of essays—there I was, a female feminist, defending the use of Foucault for feminism against a male adherent of mothering theory!—are indeed ironic, but also quite appropriate given Foucault's and my own critiques of essentialist categories.

Insofar as Balbus's critique of Foucault echoed critiques from both feminist and non-feminist social and political theorists, I used my response to it to address distortions and misunderstandings in many of the current interpretations of Foucault, and to get clearer about what using Foucault for feminism does and does not entail. I argued that contrary to prevailing assumptions, Foucault's genealogies of disciplinary power did not or, at least as I read him, should not, entail a complete rejection of psychoanalysis or any other of the disciplines that he criticized. This position was consistent with my earlier argument that a Foucauldian could consistently defend the idea of a sexual liberationist politics as long as it was neither totalistic, essentialist or ahistorical. Thus, a Foucauldian feminist could also embrace mothering theory to the extent that it was historically and culturally specific and did not claim to be the definitive account of the origins of male domination. Nevertheless, she would be more interested in a critical encounter with mothering theory that raised questions about the origins of its key concepts. In Balbus's essay mother-monopolized childrearing assumes the status of a quasi-biological given. In a genealogical vein, I ask: "When did the idea of the mother as an emotional nurturer emerge? When did the idea of women's status as reproducer prevail?"[5] Furthermore, I argue that the Foucauldian would be wary of the normalizing features of mothering theory itself. Does it unwittingly reinforce heterosexist norms? Does it overlook differences in family structure across divisions of race, class, age, and so forth?

The fourth essay in this collection, "Disciplining Mothers: Feminism and the New Reproductive Technologies," picks up on another aspect of the mothering theme, the question of new reproductive technologies. This essay represents both a meta-theoretical analysis of prevailing radical feminist critiques of these new technologies and an effort to lay out the outlines of an alternative that draws on the writings of feminists such as Linda Gordon, Rosalind Petchesky, Rayna Rapp and Donna Haraway. Both Haraway and Petchesky cite Foucault as a source for their analyses of technology and feminist reproductive politics. Like my own analyses of social and political relations, theirs emphasize resistance and ambiguity, as opposed to victimization and domination. Clearly both resistance and victimization are present; both require analysis. Indeed, feminists who appropriate Foucault fall roughly into two camps, namely, those who use his analysis of disciplinary power to isolate disciplinary technologies of women's bodies that are dominating and hence difficult to resist, and those who acknowledge domination but center on cultures of resistance to hegemonic power/knowledge formations and on how individuals who are the targets of this power can play a role in its constitution *and* its demise. Sandra Bartky and Susan Bordo offer brilliant analyses of the former type. Petchesky, Haraway, Gordon and Rapp offer the latter. Despite the fact that Foucault himself sometimes focused more on forms of domination and on the dominant discourses that constitute disciplinary technologies of the individual and the body, I have consistently linked Foucault's discourse with discourses and practices of struggle and resistance. Paradoxically, my criticism of prevailing radical feminist analyses of new reproductive technologies parallels that made by some critics of Foucault after the publication of *Discipline and Punish*.[6] They portray the power of these technologies over women's bodies such that our only options appear to be either total rejection of them or collaboration in our own domination. They also focus almost exclusively on the dominant discourses. In this essay, I offer a bifocal analysis. I acknowledge the disciplinary dimensions of the new reproductive technologies, but I also pay constant attention to the ruptures, discontinuities and cracks in the systems of power in which they are embedded. The result is an analysis of new reproductive techologies that suggests multiple strategies for resisting their dangerous implications.

"Foucault and Feminism: A Critical Reappraisal" represents an effort to respond more fully to the charges made by feminists that Foucault's discourse undermines feminism as an emancipatory project. In it, I underscore the limits of Foucault's negative concept of freedom or liberation and use remarks made by him in later interviews to argue that his project does not require us to abandon appeals to normative standards contained in traditional emancipatory theories. Finally, I address the negative impact of the domestication of Foucault in the American academy. I suggest that Foucault's emphases on self-refusal and dis-identification as practices of freedom, however important in some contexts, might subvert feminism and other oppositional movements. Thus, disidentification with his discourse becomes a necessary feature of any Foucauldian feminist appropriation of it.

The day after I submitted my dissertation for defense, I had the opportunity to sit in on a seminar with Foucault at the University of Vermont in which he was exploring the theme of "technologies of the self" for his last volumes in *The History of Sexuality*. I told him that I had just finished writing a dissertation on his critique of humanism. Not surprisingly, he responded with some embarassment and much seriousness. He suggested that I not spend energy talking about him and, instead, do what he was doing, namely, write genealogies. At the time, I remember feeling somewhat annoyed at this dismissal of the value of the project that I had just spent four years completing. The essays here collected are evidence that I did not entirely abide by his advice. I have been less preoccupied with being "true" to Foucault than with describing the contours of a viable Foucauldian feminism. I have presented the truly radical dimensions of his thought so that they might be scrutinized by a feminist audience. I have also used Foucault to intervene in highly charged issues confronting feminism in the United States. Thus, the following essays reflect my effort to think feminism through Foucault, and, where necessary, to think beyond him. They are offered so that, together, we might see what we can make of him.

1

Foucault and Feminism:
Toward a Politics of Difference

The beginning of wisdom is in the discovery that there exist contradictions of permanent tension with which it is necessary to live and that it is above all not necessary to seek to resolve.

—Andre Gorz, *Farewell to the Proletariat*

It is not difference which immobilizes us, but silence. And there are so many silences to be broken.

—Audre Lorde, *Sister Outsider*

The question of difference is at the forefront of discussions among feminists today.[1] Of course, theories of difference are not new to the women's movement. There has been much discussion concerning the nature and status of women's differences from men (for instance, biological, psychological, cultural). Theories of sexual difference have emphasized the shared experiences of women across the divisions of race, class, age or culture. In such theories the diversity of women's experiences is often lumped into the category "women's experience," or women as a class, presumably in an effort to provide the basis for a collective feminist subject.

More recently, however, as a result of experiencing conflicts at the level of practice, it is the differences among women (for instance, differences of race, class, sexual practice) that are becoming the focus of theoretical discussion. To be sure, Marxist feminists have consistently recognized the significance of class differences among women, but other important differences cry out for recognition. The question arises: do the differences and potential separations between women pose a serious threat to effective political action and to the possibility of theory?

Perhaps the most influential and provocative ideas on the issue of difference in feminism are to be found in the writings of black, lesbian feminist poet and essayist Audre Lorde. In her work,

17

Lorde describes the ways in which the differences among women have been "misnamed and misused in the service of separation and confusion."[2] As a lesbian mother and partner in an interracial couple, she has a unique insight into the conflicts and divided allegiances which put into question the possibility of a unified women's movement. She has experienced the way in which power utilizes difference to fragment opposition. Indeed this fragmentation can occur not only in groups but also within the individual. Hence, Lorde remarks: "I find I am constantly being encouraged to pluck out some one aspect of myself and present this as the meaningful whole, eclipsing or denying the other parts of self."[3]

Lorde claims that it is not the differences among women that separate us, but rather our "refusal to recognize those differences, and to examine the distortions which result from our misnaming them and their effects upon human behavior and expectation."[4] Thus, she appears to be saying that difference is not necessarily counter-revolutionary. She suggests that feminists devise ways of discovering and utilizing their differences as a source for creative change. Learning to live and struggle with many of our differences may be one of the keys to disarming the power of the white, male, middle-class norms which we have all internalized to varying degrees.

In what follows I shall elaborate on the notion of difference as resource and offer a sketch of some of the implications that what I call a "politics of difference" might have for "revolutionary" feminist theory.[5] In order to elucidate these implications I shall turn to the writings of the social philosopher and historian Michel Foucault. It is my contention that despite the androcentrism in his own writings he too has recognized the ambiguous power of difference in modern society. He recognizes that difference can be the source of fragmentation and disunity as well as a creative source of resistance and change.

My aim in this paper is twofold: (1) to turn to Foucault's work and method in order to lay out the basic features of a politics of difference; and (2) to show how such a politics might be applied in the feminist debate concerning sexuality. In order to accomplish these aims I shall begin by contrasting Foucault's politics with two existing versions of revolutionary feminism, namely, Marxist and radical feminism. I have selected these two feminist frameworks because they contain the elements of traditional revolutionary theory that Foucault is rejecting.[6] Other Foucauldian feminisms are developed by Morris and Martin.[7]

Foucault's Critique of Revolutionary Theory

It will be helpful to contrast Foucault's approach with Marxism, on the one hand, and radical feminism, on the other. Both Marxism and radical feminism conceive of historical process as a dialectical struggle for human liberation. Both have turned to history to locate the origins of oppression, and to identify a revolutionary subject. Yet, radical feminists have criticized Marxism for its inability to give an adequate account of the persistence of male domination. Replacing the category of capital, radical feminists identify patriarchy as the origin of all forms of oppression. Hence, they view the struggles of women as a sex/class as the key to human liberation.

The recent intensification of feminist attention to the differences among women might be understood as a reaction to the emergence of a body of feminist theory which attempts to represent women as a whole on the basis of little information about the diversity of women's experiences, to develop universal categories for analyzing women's oppression, and, on the basis of such analysis, to identify the most important struggles. When Audre Lorde and others speak of the importance of preserving and redefining difference, of discovering more inclusive strategies for building theory; when they speak of the need for a broad based, diverse struggle, they are calling for an alternative to a traditional revolutionary theory in which forms of oppression are either overlooked or ranked and the divisions separating women exacerbated. The question is: Are there radical alternatives to traditional revolutionary theory? As I have indicated, we can turn to Foucault for an alternative approach to understanding radical social transformation.

Foucault's is a radical philosophy without a theory of history. He does not utilize history as a means of locating a single revolutionary subject, nor does he locate power in a single material base. Nevertheless, historical research is the central component of his politics and struggle a key concept for understanding change. Accordingly, in order to evaluate the usefulness of Foucault's methods for feminism, we must first understand the historical basis of his critique of traditional revolutionary theory.

Foucault's rejection of traditional revolutionary theory is rooted in his critique of the "juridico-discursive" model of power on which it is based. This model of power underpins both liberal theories of sovereignty (that is, legitimate authority often codified in law and accompanied by a theory of rights) and Marxist theories which locate power in the economy and the state as an arm of the bourgeoisie. The juridico-discursive model of power involves three basic assumptions:

1. Power is possessed (for instance, by the individuals in the state of nature, by a class, by the people).

2. Power flows from a centralized source from top to bottom (for instance, law, the economy, the state).

3. Power is primarily repressive in its exercise (a prohibition backed by sanctions).

Foucault proposes that we think of power outside the confines of state, law or class. This enables him to locate forms of power that are obscured in traditional theories. Thus, he frees power from the domain of political theory in much the same way as radical feminists did. Rather than engage in theoretical debate with political theorists, Foucault gives historical descriptions of the different forms of power operating in the modern West. He does not deny that the juridico-discursive model of power describes one form of power. He merely thinks that it does not capture those forms of power that make centralized, repressive forms of power possible, namely, the myriad of power relations at the microlevel of society.

Foucault's own theory of power differs from the traditional model in three basic ways:

1. Power is exercised rather than possessed.

2. Power is not primarily repressive, but productive.

3. Power is analyzed as coming from the bottom up.

In what follows I shall outline Foucault's reasons for substituting his own view of power for the traditional one.

1. Foucault claims that thinking of power as a possession has led to a preoccupation with questions of legitimacy, consent and rights. (Who should possess power? When has power overstepped its limits?) Marxists have problematized consent by introducing a theory of ideology, but Foucault thinks this theory must ultimately rest on a humanistic notion of authentic consciousness as the legitimate basis of consent. Furthermore, the Marxist emphasis on power as a possession has resulted in an effort to locate those subjects in the historical field whose standpoint is potentially authentic, namely, the proletariat. Foucault suspends any reference to humanistic assumptions in his own account of power because he believes that humanism has often served more as an ideology of domination than liberation.

For the notion that power is a possession Foucault substitutes a relational model of power as exercised. By focusing on the power relations themselves, rather than on the subjects related (sovereign-subject, bourgeois-proletarian), he can give an account of how subjects are constituted by power relations.

2. This brings us to the productive nature of power. Foucault rejects the repressive model of power for two reasons. First, he thinks that if power were merely repressive, then it would be difficult to explain how it has gotten such a grip on us. Why would we continue to obey a purely repressive and coercive form of power? Indeed, repressive power represents power in its most frustrated and extreme form. The need to resort to a show of force is more often evidence of a lack of power. Second, as I have indicated, Foucault thinks that the most effective mechanisms of

power are productive. So, rather than develop a theory of history and power based on the humanistic assumption of a presocial individual endowed with inalienable rights (the liberal's state of nature), or based on the identification of an authentic human interest (Marx's species being), he gives accounts of how certain institutional and cultural practices have produced individuals. These are the practices of disciplinary power, which he associates with the rise of the human sciences in the nineteenth century.

Disciplinary power is exercised on the body and soul of individuals. It increases the power of individuals at the same time as it renders them more docile (for instance, basic training in the military). In modern society disciplinary power has spread through the production of certain forms of knowledge, such as the positivistic and hermeneutic human sciences, and through the emergence of disciplinary techniques such as techniques of surveillance, examination and discipline which facilitate the process of obtaining knowledge about individuals. Thus, ways of knowing are equated with ways of exercising power over individuals. Foucault also isolates techniques of individualization such as the dividing practices found in medicine, psychiatry, criminology, and their corresponding institutions, the hospital, asylum and prison. Disciplinary practices create the divisions healthy/ill, sane/mad, legal/delinquent, which, by virtue of their authoritative status, can be used as effective means of normalization and social control. They may involve the literal dividing off of segments of the population through incarceration or institutionalization. Usually the divisions are experienced in the society at large in more subtle ways, such as in the practice of labeling one another or ourselves as different or abnormal.

For example, in *The History of Sexuality* Foucault gives an historical account of the process through which the modern individual has come to see herself as a sexual subject. Discourses such as psychoanalysis view sexuality as the key to self-understanding and lead us to believe that in order to liberate ourselves from personality "disorders," we must uncover the truth of our sexuality. In this way dimensions of personal life are psychologized, and thus become a target for the intervention of experts.

Again, Foucault attempts to show how these discourses, and the practices based on them, have played more of a role in the normalization of the modern individual than they have in any liberatory processes. He calls for a liberation from this "government of individualization," for the discovery of new ways of understanding ourselves, new forms of subjectivity.

3. Finally, Foucault thinks that focusing on power as a possession has led to the location of power in a centralized source. For example, the Marxist location of power in a class has obscured an entire network of power relations "that invests the body, sexuality, family, kinship, knowledge, technology. . ."[8] His alternative is designed to facilitate the description of the many forms of power found outside these centralized loci. He does not deny the phenomenon of class (or state) power, he simply denies that understanding it is most important for organizing resistance. As I have indicated, Foucault expands the domain of the political to include a heterogeneous ensemble of power relations operating at the microlevel of society. The practical implication of his model is that resistance must be carried out in local struggles against the many forms of power exercised at the everyday level of social relations.

Foucault's "bottom-up" analysis of power is an attempt to show how power relations at the microlevel of society make possible certain global effects of domination, such as class power and patriarchy. He avoids using universals as explanatory concepts at the start of historical inquiry in order to prevent theoretical overreach. He states:

> One must rather conduct an ascending analysis of power starting, that is, from its infinitesimal mechanisms, which each have their own history, their own trajectory, their own tactics, and then see how these mechanisms of power have been—and continue to be—invested, colonized, utilized, involuted, transformed, displaced, extended, etc., by even more general mechanisms and by forms of global domination. It is not that this global domination extends itself right to the base in a plurality of repercussions. . .[9]

In other words, by utilizing an ascending analysis Foucault shows how mechanisms of power at the microlevel of society have become part of dominant networks of power relations. Disciplinary power was not invented by the dominant class and then extended down into the microlevel of society. It originated outside this class and was appropriated by it once it revealed its utility. Foucault is suggesting that the connection between power and the economy must be determined on the basis of specific historical analysis. It cannot be deduced from a general theory. He rejects both reductionism and functionalism insofar as the latter involves locating forms of power within a structure or institution which is self-regulating. He does not offer causal or functional explanations but rather historical descriptions of the conditions that make certain forms of domination possible. He identifies the necessary but not sufficient conditions for domination.

In short, Foucault's histories put into question the idea of a universal binary division of struggle. To be sure, such divisions do exist, but as particular and not universal historical phenomena. Of course, the corollary of his rejection of the binary model is that the notion of a subject of history, a single locus of resistance, is put into question.

Resistance

Despite Foucault's neglect of resistance in *Discipline and Punish*, in *The History of Sexuality* he defines power as dependent on resistance.[10] Moreover, emphasis on resistance is particularly evident in his more recent discussions of power and sexuality.[11]

In recent writings Foucault speaks of power and resistance in the following terms:

> Where there is power, there is a resistance, and yet, or rather consequently, this resistance is never in a position of exteriority in relation to power.[12]

> I'm not positing a substance of power. I'm simply saying: as soon as there's a relation of power there's a possibility of

resistance. We're never trapped by power: it's always possible
to modify its hold, in determined conditions and following a
precise strategy.[13]

There are two claims in the above remarks. The first is the weaker
claim that power relations are only implemented in cases where
there is resistance. In other words, power relations only arise in
cases where there is conflict, where one individual or group
wants to affect the action of another individual or group. In
addition, sometimes power enlists the resistant forces into its
own service. One of the ways it does this is by labeling them, by
establishing norms and defining differences.

The second claim implied in Foucault's description of power
is the stronger claim that wherever there is a relation of power
it is possible to modify its hold. He states: "Power is exercised
only over free subjects and only insofar as they are free."[14] Free
subjects are subjects who face a field of possibilities. Their action
is structured but not forced. Thus, Foucault does not define
power as the overcoming of resistance. When restraining forces
are overcome, power relations collapse into force relations. The
limits of power have been reached.

So, while Foucault has been accused of describing a totalitarian power from which there is no escape, he denies that "there is
a primary and fundamental principle of power which dominates
society down to the smallest detail."[15] At the same time he claims
that power is everywhere. He describes the social field as a
myriad of unstable and heterogeneous relations of power. It is
an open system which contains possibilities of domination as
well as resistance.

Foucault describes the social and historical field as a battle-
field, a field of struggle. Power circulates in this field and is
exercised on and by individuals over others as well as themselves.
When speaking of struggle, he refuses to identify the subjects of
struggle. When asked the question: "Who is struggling against
whom?" he responds:

This is just a hypothesis, but I would say it's all against all.
There aren't immediately given subjects of a struggle, one

the proletariat, the other the bourgeoisie. Who fights against whom? We all fight against each other. And there is always within each of us something that fights something else.[16]

Depending on where one is and in what role (for instance, mother, lover, teacher, anti-racist, anti-sexist) one's allegiances and interests will shift. There are no privileged or fundamental coalitions in history, but rather a series of unstable and shifting ones.

In his theory of resistant subjectivity Foucault opens up the possibility of something more than a history of constructions or of victimization. That is, he opens the way for a historical knowledge of struggles. His genealogical method is designed to facilitate an "insurrection of subjugated knowledges." These are forms of knowledge or experience that "have been disqualified as inadequate to their task, or insufficiently elaborated: naive knowledges, located low down in the hierarchy, beneath the required level of cognition or scientificity."[17] They include the low-ranking knowledge ("popular knowledge") of the psychiatric patient, the hysteric, the imprisoned criminal, the housewife, the indigent. Popular knowledge is not shared by all people, "but it is, on the contrary, a particular, local, regional knowledge, a *differential* knowledge incapable of unanimity."[18]

The question whether some forms of resistance are more effective than others is a matter of social and historical investigation and not of a priori theoretical pronouncement. The basis for determining which alliances are politically viable ought not to be an abstract principle of unity, but rather historical and contextual analysis of the field of struggle. Thus feminism can mobilize individuals from diverse sites in the social field and thereby use differences as a resource.[19]

Genealogy as a Form of Resistance

Foucault introduces genealogical critique as his alternative to traditional revolutionary theory. He attempts to liberate us from the oppressive effects of prevailing modes of self-understanding inherited through the humanist tradition. As one commentator suggests, for Foucault, "Freedom does not basically lie in discovering or being able to determine who we are, but in rebelling against those ways in which we are already defined, categorized, and classified."[20] Moreover, the view that a theory of history should enable us to control history is part of the Enlightenment legacy from which Foucault is attempting to "free" us. For him, there is no theory of global transformation to formulate, no revolutionary subject whose interest the intellectual or theoretician can represent. He recommends an alternative to the traditional role for the intellectual in modern political struggles. He speaks of the "specific intellectual" in contrast to the "universal intellectual," that is, the "bearer of universal values" who represents the enlightened consciousness of a revolutionary subject.

The specific intellectual operates with a different conception of the relation between theory and practice:

> Intellectuals have gotten used to working, not in the modality of the "universal," the "exemplary," the "just-and- true-for all," but within specific sectors, at the precise points where their own conditions of life or work situate them (housing, the hospital, the asylum, the laboratory, the university, family and social relations).[21]

Focusing attention on specific situations may lead to more concrete analyses of particular struggles and thus to a better understanding of social change. For example, Foucault was involved in certain conflicts within medicine, psychiatry and the penal system. He devised ways for prisoners to participate in discussions of prison reform. His history of punishment was designed to alter our perspectives on the assumptions that inform penal practices.

In part, Foucault's refusal to make any universal political, or moral, judgments is based on the historical evidence that what looks like a change for the better may have undesirable consequences. Since struggle is continual and the idea of a power-free society is an abstraction, those who struggle must never grow complacent. Victories are often overturned; changes may take on different faces over time. Discourses and institutions are ambiguous and may be utilized for different ends.

So Foucault is in fact pessimistic about the possibility of controlling history. But this pessimism need not lead to despair. Only a disappointed traditional revolutionary would lapse into fatalism at the thought that much of history is out of our control. Foucault's emphasis on resistance is evidence that he is not fatalistic himself, but merely skeptical about the possibilities of global transformation. He has no particular utopian vision. Yet, one need not have an idea of utopia in order to take seriously the injustices in the present. Furthermore, the past has provided enough examples of theoretical inadequacy to make Foucault's emphasis on provisional theoretical reflection reasonable.

In short, genealogy as resistance involves using history to give voice to the marginal and submerged voices which lie "a little beneath history"—the voices of the mad, the delinquent, the abnormal, the disempowered. It locates many discontinuous and regional struggles against power both in the past and present. These voices are the sources of resistance, the creative subjects of history.[22]

Foucault and Feminism: Toward a Politics of Difference

What are the implications of Foucault's critique of traditional revolutionary theory, his use of history and his analysis of power for feminism? I have called Foucault's politics a politics of difference because it does not assume that all differences can be bridged. Neither does it assume that difference must be an obstacle to effective resistance. Indeed, in a politics of difference, difference can be a resource insofar as it enables us to multiply the sources of resistance to particular forms of domination and to discover distortions in our understandings of each other and the world. In a politics of difference, as Audre Lorde suggests, redefining our differences, learning from them, becomes the central task.

Of course, it may be that Lorde does envision the possibility of some underlying commonality, some universal humanity, which will provide the foundation for an ultimate reconciliation of our differences. Her own use of the concept of the "erotic" might be understood as an implicit appeal to humanism.[23] As we have seen, Foucault's method requires a suspension of humanistic assumptions. Indeed, feminists have recognized the dangers of what Adrienne Rich refers to as "the urge to leap across feminism to 'human liberation.' "[24] What Foucault offers to feminism is not a humanist theory, but rather a critical method which is thoroughly historical and a set of recommendations about how to look at our theories. The motivation for a politics of difference is the desire to avoid dogmatic adherence to categories and assumptions as well as the elision of differences to which such dogmatism can lead.

In conclusion, I want to illustrate the value and limitations of Foucault's politics of difference by bringing it to bear on a recent discussion of difference within feminism, namely, the sexuality debate. This debate has polarized American feminists into two groups, radical and libertarian feminists.[25] The differences being discussed threaten to destroy communications between them. Hence, an understanding of their differences is crucial at this conjuncture in American feminism.

Radical feminists condemn any sexual practices involving the "male" ideology of sexual objectification which, in their view, underlies both male sexual violence and the institutionalization of masculine and feminine roles in the patriarchal family. They call for an elimination of all patriarchal institutions in which sexual objectification occurs, such as pornography, prostitution, compulsory heterosexuality, sadomasochism, cruising, adult/ child and butch/femme relations. They substitute an emphasis on intimacy and affection for the "male" preoccupation with sexual pleasure.

In contrast, libertarian feminists attack radicals for having succumbed to sexual repression. Since radicals believe that sex as we know it is male, they are suspicious of any sexual relations whatsoever. Libertarians stress the dangers of censoring any sexual practices between consenting partners and recommend the transgression of socially acceptable sexual norms as a strategy of liberation.

What is remarkable about these debates from the perspective of a Foucauldian politics of difference is the extent to which the two camps share similar views of power and freedom. In both camps, power is represented as centralized in key institutions which dictate the acceptable terms of sexual expression, namely, male-dominated heterosexual institutions whose elements are crystallized in the phenomenon of pornography on the one hand, and all discourses and institutions that distinguish legitimate from illegitimate sexual practice (including radical feminism) thereby creating a hierarchy of sexual expression, on the other. Moreover, both seem to regard sexuality as a key arena in the struggle for human liberation. Thus, for both, understanding the truth about sexuality is central for liberation.

In addition, both operate with repressive models of power. Radical feminists are in fact suspicious of all sexual practices insofar as they view sexual desire as a male construct. They think male sexuality has completely repressed female sexuality and that we must eliminate the source of this repression, namely, all heterosexual male institutions, before we can begin to construct our own. Libertarians explicitly operate with a repressive model of power borrowed from the Freudo-Marxist discourses of Wilhelm Reich and Herbert Marcuse. They recognize that women's sexual expression has been particularly repressed in our society and advocate women's right to experiment with their sexuality. They resist drawing any lines between safe and dangerous, politically correct and politically incorrect sex. Radical feminists accuse libertarians of being male identified because they have not problematized sexual desire; libertarians accuse radicals of being traditional female sex-prudes.

There are other similarities between the two camps. In the first place, as Ann Ferguson has pointed out, both involve universalist theories of sexuality, that is, they both reify "male" and "female" sexuality and thus fail to appreciate that sexuality is a historically and culturally specific construct.[26] This is problematic insofar as it assumes that there is some essential connection between gender and sexual practice. An historical understanding of sexuality would attempt to disarticulate gender and sexuality and thereby reveal the diversity of sexual experiences across gender as well as other divisions. For example, Rennie Simpson suggests that African American women's sexuality has been constructed differently from white women's.[27] They have a strong tradition of self-reliance and sexual self-determination. Thus, for American black women, the significance of the sexuality debates may be different. Indeed, the relationship between violence and sexuality takes on another dimension when viewed in the light of past uses of lynching to control black male sexuality. And consider the significance of women of color's emphasis on issues such as forced sterilization or dumping Depo Provera on third-world countries over that of white American feminists on abortion on demand.[28] Yet, radical feminists still tend to focus on dominant culture and the victimization of women. Ann Snitow and Carol Vance clearly identify the problem with this approach when they remark:

> To ignore the potential for variations (in women's sexual expression) is inadvertently to place women outside the culture except as passive recipients of official systems of symbols. It continues to deny what mainstream culture has always tried to make invisible—the complex struggles of disenfranchised groups to grapple with oppression using symbolic as well as economic and political resistance.[29]

Rather than generalize on the basis of the stereotypes provided by "dominant culture," feminists must explore the meaning of the diversity of sexual practices to those who practice them, to resurrect the "subjugated knowledge" of sexuality elided within dominant culture.

Secondly, both radicals and libertarians tend to isolate sexuality as the key cause of women's oppression. Therefore, they locate power in a central source and identify a universal strategy for seizing control of sexuality (for instance, eliminate pornography, transgress sexual taboos by giving expression to sexual desire). Both of these analyses are simplistic and reductionist. While it is important, sexuality is simply one of the many areas of everyday life in which power operates.

In sum, the critique of the sexuality debates developed out of a politics of difference amounts to (1) a call for more detailed research into the diverse range of women's sexual experiences; and (2) avoiding analyses that invoke universal explanatory categories or a binary model of oppression and that thereby overlook the many differences in women's experience of sexuality.

Although a politics of difference does not offer feminists a morality derived from a universal theory of oppression, it need not lapse into a form of pluralism in which anything goes. On the basis of specific theoretical analyses of particular struggles, one can make generalizations, identify patterns in relations of power and thereby identify the relative effectiveness or ineffectiveness, safety or danger of particular practices. For example, a series of links have been established between the radical feminist strategy of anti-pornography legislation and the New Right's efforts to censor any sexual practices that pose a threat to the family. This is not to suggest that the anti-pornography movement is essentially reactionary, but rather that at this time it may be dangerous. Similarly, one ought not to assume that there is any necessary connection between transgression of sexual taboos and sexual liberation. Denying that censorship is the answer to patriarchal sexual oppression is not tantamount to endorsing any particular form of transgression as liberatory.

In a feminist politics of difference, theory and moral judgments are geared to specific contexts. This need not preclude systematic analysis of the present, but it does require that our categories be provisional. As Snitow and Vance point out: "We need to live with the uncertainties that arise along with the change we desire."[30] What is certain is that our differences are ambiguous; they may be used either to divide us or to enrich our politics. If we are not the ones to give voice to them, then history suggests that they will continue to be either misnamed and distorted, or simply reduced to silence.[31]

2

Identity Politics and Sexual Freedom

At a time when attention to differences among women is at the forefront of feminist discussion, differences concerning sexual behavior and politics have produced particularly heated debates within feminism. The sexuality debates that have been raging for over four years now have increasingly led to a polarization of American feminists into two camps, radical and libertarian.[1] Some have stayed above the fray, watching with impatience and skepticism believing that the debates are a red herring or a self-indulgent diversion from more important struggles. Others, myself among them, have watched with interest. Not a prurient interest, but one sparked by the conviction that the debates have exposed certain lacunae in feminist theory.

In particular, they have brought to light inadequacies in current feminist conceptions of power and freedom, and confusion (even "crisis") over what constitutes membership in the "feminist community." Yet the debates have been productive insofar as they have redirected feminist attention to two important questions. What is (or ought to be) the relationship of feminism to struggles for sexual liberation, that is, to sexual identity politics? What are the implications of the differences among women for building a unified feminist theory and practice?

In a recent issue of *Signs* Ann Ferguson has attempted to move debate forward by offering a constructive critique of the concepts of freedom, power and sexuality that underlie the positions of both camps.[2] She is part of an emerging third position that rejects the division between radical and libertarian feminists as exhaustive. I too want to contribute to the movement beyond polarized debate by further developing the theoretical and practical implications of a more adequate "sexual politics" in the recent work of Michel Foucault. Although Foucault is sometimes described as a libertarian himself, his analysis of power and sexuality can provide the basis for a sexual politics that escapes between the Scylla of a moralistic dogmatism and the Charybdis of a libertarian pluralism in which anything goes.[3]

Sexual Freedom and Sexual Repression

Ann Ferguson offers a useful sketch of the two paradigms of sexual freedom that inform the sexuality debates. According to Ferguson, radical feminists assert that

> Sexual freedom requires the sexual equality of partners and their equal respect for one another as both subject and body. It also requires the elimination of all patriarchal institutions (e.g., the pornography industry, the patriarchal family, prostitution, and compulsory heterosexuality), and sexual practices (sadomasochism, cruising, adult/child and butch/femme relationships) in which sexual objectification occurs.[4]

In contrast, libertarian feminists assert that

> Sexual freedom requires oppositional practices, that is, transgressing socially respectable categories of sexuality and refusing to draw the line on what counts as politically correct sexuality.[5]

What I find remarkable about these definitions, and the many particular positions from which they are abstracted, is what they have in common. As we shall see, both involve repressive models of power. Moreover, both locate power in a key institution or group of individuals. Indeed, a more careful look reveals two distinct versions of repression, which I will refer to as the traditional repressive hypothesis and the social constructionist repressive hypothesis.

The Traditional Repressive Hypothesis

Feminist commentators have frequently addressed the naturalist and biological determinist tendency in radical feminist theory.[6] Such tendencies are particularly evident in their attribution of male dominance to male biology and their identification of femininity with women's biological role in procreation.[7] Thus, they appeal to a form of essentialism in which "male sexuality" is associated with violence, lust, objectification and a preoccupation with orgasm; and "female sexuality" with nurturance, reciprocity, intimacy and an emphasis on non-genital pleasure. Accordingly, sexual freedom is construed negatively, as freedom from male dominated institutions whose elements are crystallized in pornography, particularly its sadomasochistic varieties. In patriarchal societies like our own female sexuality can presumably flourish only in isolated and marginal contexts, such as egalitarian lesbian relationships. In short, a natural and inherently good female sexuality is portrayed as repressed by a male sexuality based on coercion and violence against women. Sexual freedom requires the restraint of male sexuality as we know it, or its elimination altogether.

Some libertarians have also appealed to the notion of a repressed, natural and innocent sexuality.[8] They borrow this model from the sexual liberationist instinct/control paradigm rooted in Freudian psychology and found in the writings of more recent sexologists from Reich and Marcuse to Masters and Johnson. In this view, the basic difference between male and female sexuality is that the latter is more repressed. For example, while all libertarian feminists acknowledge sexism in pornography, they regard the release of female sexual energy as more important than the restraint of male sexuality. Therefore, they resist drawing lines between safe and dangerous, politically correct and incorrect sex. The primary obstacle to sexual freedom, according to this view, is the existence of normative hierarchies of sexual expression that inhibit the release of an inherently liberatory (or benign) sexual energy. Again, as in the radical feminist's accounts, we find a negative view of freedom—freedom is freedom from repressive norms.

The difficulties with the traditional repressive hypothesis and its concomitant versions of sexual freedom have often been pointed out. In the first place, it is ahistorical, that is, it fails to address the social and historical construction of sexual desire and behavior, and the dialectical character of the relationship between biology and culture.[9] Moreover, insofar as radical feminists universalize "male" and "female" sexuality, they fail to account for sexual diversity across divisions of race, class, age, and the like. Libertarians fall into the same ahistoricity, naturalism and essentialism by default when they accuse radicals of a "female" sex prudishness and fail to explore how desires are constructed in the context of patriarchal and capitalist social relations. Finally, both groups fail to identify a positive model of sexual freedom in the present. Many radicals are asking us to wait until male controlled sexuality has been overthrown. Libertarians offer an inadequate account of the dangers that accompany female sexual exploration in a sexist society.

The Social Constructionist Repressive Hypothesis

Not all radical and libertarian feminists operate with the instinct/control model of sexual repression presented above. To be sure, the feminist sexuality debates have reflected the influence of recent work in the history of sexuality that rejects the idea of an autonomous sexual drive.[10] Members of both camps speak of the social construction of desire.[11]

Ironically, essentialist tendencies that plague naturalistic accounts of sexual repression sometimes reappear in social constructionism. One obvious difference in the latter is the recognition that desire can be transformed. Nevertheless, as philosopher Sandra Bartky has pointed out, feminists lack an adequate "politics of personal transformation".[12] How one goes about altering one's desires when they appear to conflict with "feminist" political or moral principles is not obvious. Nor is the extent to which such desires can be consciously altered at all clear. What should be clear in any social constructionist account of sexual desire is that the naturalistic recourse to an innocent or malevolent desire is inadequate. So, too, is a retreat into liberal arguments about the sanctity of private life. (Indeed, one of the strengths of radical feminism has been its consistent rejection of such strategies.) These strategies fail to analyze the degree to which sexuality is both a target of oppression and an arena of political struggle with liberatory potential.

Radical feminists who acknowledge that desire is socially constructed still operate with a model of power as centralized in male institutions and as possessed by men. Hence, they regard male control of the modes of reproduction as the most fundamental form of oppression and call for women to seize control of the material base of patriarchy in order to effect revolution. An adaptation of this model to the issue of sexual freedom is found in the following statement by Karen Rian in her article, "Sadomasochism and the Social Construction of Desire":

> Since our sexuality has been constructed for the most part through social structures over which we have had no control, we all "consent" to sexual desires and activities which are alienating to at least some degree. However, there is a vast difference between consent and self-determination. The latter includes the former, but in addition entails *control over the social structures which shape our lives,* including our sexual desires and relationships. . . . [S]exual liberation involves the freedom to redefine and reconstruct our sexuality, which in turn reshapes our sexual desires.[13]

What is undesirable about Rian's understanding of sexual freedom is its sex-negativity and totalistic view of power. According to Rian, sexual self-determination is possible only if women control the social structures that shape their lives—in other words, after the feminist revolution. This is a utopian conception of freedom that has nihilistic consequences for the present. Here radical change consists in the complete negation of present sexual relations. The ambiguity and multiplicity of current sexual practices are effectively denied and social transformation is detemporalized.[14]

Furthermore, although Rian herself acknowledges that *all* of us are sexually alienated to some degree, other radical feminists have tended to focus exclusively on the construction of female desire, particularly the desires of females whose sexual behaviors are regarded as more suspect, for example, lesbian sadomasochists and butch/femme couples. The result is an overemphasis on the victimization of women and a portrayal of them as passive containers of male sexual ideology. The picture of history that emerges in this view reflects little struggle and leads to little hope of radical social transformation. Nor does this picture of female containment by male domination offer an account of deviance from the male-defined norms. How are "feminist" sexual practices possible in male-dominated society? Finally, the process through which *male desire* has been constructed remains unanalyzed. We are left to surmise that an unalienated and monolithic male desire is actually reflected in the current system. Again, the argument rests on covert essentialist premises.

A more promising direction for future thinking about sexuality, feminism, power and freedom within the social constructionist framework may be developed from the writings of radical social theorist and historian Michel Foucault. Foucault offers an analysis of sexuality and power that, in the words of Foucauldian feminist Gayle Rubin, "recognizes repressive phenomena without resorting to the language of libido."[15] Foucault does not deny that there is sexual repression, but rather shifts attention to a larger set of productive power relations operating throughout the social body which constitute us as the subjects of modern sexual experience.

It is by now well-known that, according to Foucault, power has not operated primarily by denying sexual expression but by creating the forms that modern sexuality takes. In the *History of Sexuality,* he describes a process through which sexuality in the twentieth century came to be understood as a key to self-understanding and human liberation. Through this deployment of sexuality, sex became a target for intervention into family life by medical, psychiatric and governmental experts whose discourses and practices create the divisions healthy/ill, normal/perverse, legal/criminal, and carry an authoritative status enabling them to be utilized as effective means of social control. However, Foucault's interests do not lie only in analyzing the power of experts. More importantly, he examines the maintenance of social control through a marginalization and medicalization of "deviancy" that diverts attention from tolerated "abnormalities" within "normal" social intercourse. (One might analyze marital rape or white collar crime along these lines.) Rather than treat the history of sexuality as a history of the imposing or lifting of restrictions on sexual expression, Foucault describes how power has produced our ways of understanding and taking up sexual practices and how these discourses later become the primary positions in struggles concerning sexuality, thereby eliding the reality of other experiences and practices.

Thus, Foucault rejects Reich's science-based sexual liberationist claims that saying yes to sex is saying no to power. This is not an endorsement of sadomasochism, but, rather, the claim that relaxing restraints on sexual expression is not inherently liberatory. Foucault shifts our attention away from a preoccupation with "repression" as the central concept for analyzing the relationship between sex and power.

In effect, Foucault claims that individuals have been repressed *through* sexuality, particularly through the production of discourses in the human sciences and the practices associated with them, but also in our own everyday practices. "Repression" refers to efforts to control socially constructed desires. In fact, Foucault claims that deviancy is controlled and norms are established through the very process of identifying the deviant as such, then observing it, further classifying it, monitoring and "treating" it. Hence, as some gays and lesbians achieve a modicum of acceptance in the contemporary United States, new norms have been established within these groups through the identification of deviant practices that are relative to theirs. We have here another example of what Foucault refers to as the "deployment of sexuality." Accordingly, he recommends that we "desexualize" the contemporary political domain and has endorsed feminist strategies which do just that. For example, when questioned concerning strategies for sexual liberation, Foucault replied:

> What I want to make apparent is precisely that the object "sexuality" is in reality an instrument formed long ago, and one which has constituted a centuries-long apparatus of subjection. The real strength of the women's movement is not that of having laid claim to the specificity of their sexuality and the rights pertaining to it, but that they have actually departed from the discourse conducted within the apparatuses of sexuality. . . . [This constitutes] a veritable de-sexualization, a displacement effected in relation to the sexual centering of the problem, formulating the demand for forms of culture, discourse, language . . . which are no longer part of that rigid assignation and pinning down to their sex.[16]

Thus, when feminists expand the domain of sexuality to include issues such as abortion and reproduction, they engage in a desexualization of their struggles and move away from gender-based identity politics. In contrast, homosexual liberation movements have been (understandably) "caught at the level of demands for the right to their sexuality."[17]

At this point it might seem that Foucault's work would provide an unlikely source of support for radical sexual liberationism. Foucault's comments on de-sexualizing political struggle do seem to put into question the viability of sexual struggles centering on individual's attachments to their sexual identities, for example, homosexual, sadomasochist, fetishist, and so forth. In other words, Foucault does sometimes speak as though the domain of sexuality were already colonized beyond redemption.

It is essential to clarify the nature of Foucault's misgivings concerning liberation struggles rooted in identity politics in order to avoid misunderstanding. In effect he has described a form of domination that operates by categorizing individuals and attaching them to their identities, a form of power that locates the truth of the individual in his or her sexuality. Hence, it is not surprising that he would be skeptical about a strategy for liberation founded on the very discourses he has attempted to debunk, namely the discourses of medicine and psychiatry that emerged in the nineteenth century. These discourses located identity within the psyche or body of the individual, conceiving of the latter as a fixed and unified entity. Gays and lesbians today still appeal to this notion of identity when they describe their own sexualities as "orientations", as a matter of how they were born, rather than "preferences." In contrast to this static and individualistic model of identity is one that views personal identity as constituted by the myriad of social relationships and practices in which the individual is engaged. Because these relationships are sometimes contradictory and often unstable, the identity that emerges is fragmented and dynamic. Thus, for example, in a racist and homophobic society, a black lesbian experiences the conflicting aspects of her identity in terms of conflicts over loyalties and interests relative to the black and lesbian communities. In the same way, lesbian feminists involved in butch/femme role-playing experience conflicting loyalties.

In this view of the self, the relationship between the individual and society is not pictured as one of social determination or complete socialization. Socialization, rather, emerges as a theoretical project that is never fully realized in practice. Therefore, social constructionism need not imply social determinism. Foucault's certainly does not.

In the above account of the construction of personal identity, the notion of the individual's interests also becomes problematic. As Ann Ferguson aptly states:

> In a situation where various important aspects of one's identity is ongoing social practices lead one to define contrary interests in relation to different groups, an individual cannot

> simply accept the social practices and the interests defined
> through them, as given.[18]

In such a relational view of personal identity, one's interests are a function of one's place in the social field at a particular time, not given. They are constantly open to change and contestation.

Indeed, individuals experiencing such conflicts are in an especially good position to understand the desireable features of coalition politics. Coalitions provide an opportunity for individuals who experience some of the privileges of dominant groups to redefine how they differ from individuals in subordinate groups. Moreover, those in subordinate groups can come to appreciate how it is possible for someone who is dominant in some, but not all, respects to share their interests.[19]

An understanding of sexual liberation based on this latter notion of identity, one that is a product of social relations and conflicts, requires more than the demand for a right to one's sexuality; for, on this model, one's "sexuality" is a matter of socially and historically specific practices and relationships that are contingent and dynamic, and thus a matter of political struggle. In such a model of identity, freedom does not follow from a notion of one's true nature or essence as "human being," "woman," "homosexual" or "proletarian." It is rather our capacity to choose the forms of experience through which we constitute ourselves.[20]

Foucault's skepticism concerning struggles for sexual liberation must also be understood in the light of his rejection of totalizing theories that prescribe universal strategies for human liberation on the basis of essentialist sciences of sexuality, or the economy, or the "libidinal economy." Essentialist humanisms obscure the irreducible plurality of habits, practices, experiences and desires within the many different sexual subcultures. Foucault wants to avoid the dominating features of the universalism implicit in such humanisms and the elision of difference to which they lead. According to Foucault, there are many sides to political struggles for social transformation. Indeed, as we have seen, struggle goes on within and between subjects.

While Foucault's analysis of sexual identity is not sufficient to reject radical sexual politics, neither should it be the basis for rejecting coalitions with sex radicals. Following the example of Foucault's analysis of the history of the power to punish in *Discipline and Punish,* Gayle Rubin has recommended that we displace the categories of thought about sexuality from "the more traditional ones of sin, disease, neurosis, pathology . . . [etc.]" (those that Foucault has described as part of the deployment of sexuality), to "populations, neighborhoods, settlement patterns, migration, urban conflict, epidemiology, and police technology."[21] She thus calls for detailed analyses of the relationships between "stigmatized erotic populations and the social forces which regulate them," in order to bring into focus the particular forms of oppression that sex radicals face.[22]

Furthermore, Foucault himself provides justification for continuing to struggle at the level of sexual politics when he acknowledges that discourse is ambiguous. His most recent remarks about discourse, power, and resistance make it clear that there is no final word concerning the political status of sexual struggles—even those based on sexual identity. Foucault defines discourse as a form of power that circulates in the social field and can attach to strategies of domination as well as to those of resistance. Neither wholly a source of domination nor of resistance, sexuality is also neither outside power nor wholly circumscribed by it. Instead, it is itself an arena of struggle. There are no inherently liberatory or repressive sexual practices, for any practice is cooptable and any capable of becoming a source of resistance. After all, if relations of power are dispersed and fragmented throughout the social field, so must resistance to power be. Evaluating the political status of sexual practices should be a matter of historical and social investigation and not a priori theoretical pronouncement.

Finally, according to this analysis of power and resistance, freedom lies in our capacity to discover the historical links between certain modes of self-understanding and modes of domination, and to resist the ways in which we have already been classified and identified by dominant discourses. This means discovering new ways of understanding ourselves and each other, refusing to accept the dominant cultures' characterizations of our practices and desires, and redefining them from within resistant cultures.

Lesbian feminists have certainly been effective at such reconceiving. But their new self-understandings are not immune to cooptation within dominant power relations. For example, lesbian feminists could be tempted to capitulate to more conservative forces by disavowing their affiliation with other oppressed sexual minorities rather than engaging in efforts to further articulate their connections with the sex fringe. One way to achieve the latter would be to engage in a process of collective consciousness-raising. This would require that we continue to provide detailed historical analyses of the ways in which sexuality has become a pivotal target in strategies of domination. The purpose of such consciousness-raising would not be to tell us who we are, but rather to free us from certain ways of understanding ourselves; that is, to tell us who we do not have to be and to tell us how we came to think of ourselves as we do.

Beyond Dogmatism and Liberal Pluralism

There are several advantages to this Foucauldian analysis of power and freedom. In the first place, like radical feminist theory, it politicizes the personal domain and thereby avoids the liberal trap of conceiving of our personal desires and relationships as outside power. But unlike radical feminist theory, it does not locate power in a monolithic structure or central institution such as pornography or compulsory heterosexuality. This should be desirable to radical feminists who learned from their experiences with leftists in the sixties how oppressive the economic reductionism of gender issues could be. At that time personal politics were not only given a low priority, but were treated as self-indulgent and bourgeois. The recent radical feminist position on sexual freedom, which requires that women control the modes of reproduction before they can determine their sexuality, parallels early Marxist skepticism about radical transformation in the personal domain until after the revolution.

A second advantage of this analysis is that it enables us to think of difference as a resource rather than a threat. In another paper I have developed more fully the idea of a "politics of difference."[23] In a politics of difference one is not always attempting to overcome difference. One does not regard difference as an obstacle to effective resistance. Difference can be a resource insofar as it enables us to multiply the sources of resistance to the many relations of domination that circulate through the social field. If there is no central locus of power, then neither is there a central locus of resistance. Moreover, if we redefine our differences, discover new ways of understanding ourselves and each other, then our differences are less likely to be used against us. In short, a politics that is designed to avoid dogmatism in our categories and politics, as well as the silencing of difference to which such dogmatism can lead, is a welcome alternative to polarized debate. Dialogue between women with different sexual preferences can be opened, not with the aim of eliminating these differences, but rather of learning from them and discovering the basis for coalition building. Of course, this means discovering what we have in common as well. We need not universalize difference either. In this view our basis for common struggle is a democratic and provisional one, subject to recreation and renegotiation.[24]

Only if feminists democratize their struggles by giving equal respect to the claims of other oppressed minorities will they avoid what Richard Sennett once described as "destructive *Gemeinschaft*."[25] Destructive *Gemeinschaft* refers to the destructive sense of community in which conflict is experienced as an "all or nothing contest for personal legitimacy," that is, for the right to have one's feelings.[26] Individuals involved in such conflicts sometimes become preoccupied more with bolstering their own identities than with their political goals. Such identity politics can be self-defeating insofar as they often lead to internal struggles over who really belongs to the community. I fear that Sennett aptly characterizes the current situation within a part of the feminist movement when he remarks: "Powerlessness comes from the very attempts to define a collective identity instead of defining the common interests of a diverse group of people.[27] At its best, feminism has been very effective at realizing methods for sharing feelings in order to foster shared political commitment. We need to return to this model of consciousness-raising in order to learn from our differences and use them to enrich our politics. In addition, if we recognize that identities are historically constituted, then we can accept their contingency. We might even be prepared for the dissolution of feminism or lesbianism as we understand them in the future and thus not attach ourselves to our identities so rigidly. I am not suggesting that we can will them away, but rather that we might be more effective if we become less concerned with preserving them or imposing them on others and more concerned with eliminating injustices wherever they arise. Furthermore, the differences among women could be productive insofar as they stimulate a wide variety of visions for the future.

A final advantage of Foucault's mode of analysis is that it politicizes theory as well. He often highlighted the oppressive practical consequences of humanistic revolutionary or liberal political theories. Again, Gayle Rubin follows his example when she points to the limits of her own totalistic analysis of the "sex/gender system" as she developed it in her landmark essay, "The Traffic in Women."[28] There she treated gender and sexual desire as systematically connected. In her most recent work she provides a methodological framework for exploring other structures, other power relations in which sexuality is enmeshed. In other words, she no longer believes that sexuality is wholly a product of the gender system. She believes it is a mistake to view feminism as capable of providing the ultimate and total account of social oppression.

Foucault also stressed the specificity and the autonomy of the many modes of oppression in modern society. He emphasized the fragmented and open-ended character of the social field. Therefore, he was skeptical about the possibility and desirability of grand theory. Rather than offer one himself, he subjected modern theories in psychology or criminology, as well as Marxist and liberal political theories, to historical reflection in an effort to render them problematic in the present. He described the roles that they have played in practices of domination and oppression. Given his skepticism about grand theory, and his emphasis on the heterogeneity and fragmentation of the social field, he is led to a theoretical pluralism of sorts. For if difference is distorted and obscured in totalistic theories, the obvious path for resistance to take is to provide alternative mappings of specific regions of the social field. In other words, theoretical pluralism makes possible the expansion of social ontology, a redefinition and redescription of experience from the perspectives of those who are more often simply objects of theory. Feminists have begun to provide new maps. Sexually oppressed minorities can provide others.

Of course, on the basis of specific theoretical analyses one can make generalizations, identify links between forms of oppression, and locate patterns of domination. Thus, one can evaluate the relative practical values and dangers of particular tactics of resistance. But this represents a very different understanding of the role of theory from that promulgated by Freudian, Marxist and feminist humanists. Foucault's theories do not tell us what to do, but rather how some of our ways of thinking and doing are historically linked to particular forms of power and social control. His theories serve less to explain than to criticize and raise questions. His histories of theory are designed to reveal their contingency and thereby free us from them.

To be sure, there is an element of pessimism in all of this. In the first place, the call for theoretical and practical pluralism is based on the implicit assumption that a power-free society is an abstraction and struggle, a ubiquitous feature of history. Those engaged in struggle can expect the changes they bring about to take on a different face over time. Discourses and institutions are ambiguous and may be utilized for different ends. Secondly, and correlatively, a Foucauldian sexual politics does not aspire to control history or to bring about global transformation all at once. There is no single vision of life "after the revolution." Yet, one need not have an idea of utopia to recognize and struggle against injustices in the present. And if there is a vision of the future implicit in this approach, it is one of a democratic and heterogeneous society.

The history of sexual politics over the past 150 years has provided enough examples of theoretical and strategic inadequacy to make a theoretical and practical pluralism reasonable. This need not be a pluralism in which anything goes. In fact, it would be more appropriately described as a "pluralism in which nothing goes," that is, one in which everything is potentially dangerous.[29] In one of the last interviews before his untimely death Foucault remarked: "My point is not that everything is bad, but that everything is dangerous."[30] Foucault's own reluctance to be explicit about his ethical and political positions is attributable not to nihilism, relativism or political irresponsibility, but rather to his sense of the dangers of political programs based on grand theory.

Thus, turning to Foucault in our efforts to analyze the recent debates between radical and libertarian feminists does not answer the question "What should be done?" But if we reflect seriously on the lessons of the sexuality debates, a few conclusions concerning what could be avoided do emerge. Foucault's analyses of power and sexuality put into question the viability of using essentialist notions of sexual identity as a basis for building a feminist theory and politics. Moreover, they have highlighted the importance of keeping open the question "Which desires are liberating?" Indeed, they raise doubts about the possibility or desirability of ever giving a final answer to this question. Finally, they point to the need to subject our feminist categories and concepts to critical historical analysis in a continual effort to expose their limitations and highlight their specificity. Perhaps the least dangerous way to discover whether and how specific practices are enslaving or liberating us is not to silence and exclude differences, but rather to use them to diversify and renegotiate the arena of radical political struggle.[31]

3

Feminism and the Power of Foucauldian Discourse: Foucault and Mothering Theory

Is Foucauldian feminism a contradiction in terms? I would not have thought so. After all, Foucault and feminists both focus upon sexuality as a key arena of political struggle. Both expand the domain of the "political" to include forms of social domination associated with the personal sphere. And both launch critiques against forms of biological determinism, and humanism. Finally, both are skeptical of the human sciences insofar as the latter have been implicated in modern forms of domination. Indeed, rather than link the growth of knowledge with progress, both describe how the growth of specific forms of knowledge— for instance in medicine, psychiatry, sociology, psychology—has been linked to the emergence of subtle mechanisms of social control, and to the elision of other forms of knowledge and experience.[1]

Yet, as focused as Foucault was on domains of power/knowledge in which many of the bodies disciplined and the subjects produced and rendered docile were female, he never spoke of "male domination" per se; he usually spoke of power as if it subjugated everyone equally. As feminist critic Sandra Bartky, who is sympathetic to Foucault, rightly points out: "To overlook the forms of subjection that engender the feminine body is to perpetuate the silence and powerlessness of those upon whom these disciplines have been imposed."[2]

49

This charge of androcentrism notwithstanding, Bartky, myself, and many other feminists have found Foucault's discourses and methods useful tools for feminist criticism.[3] Moreover, in the first volume of his *History of Sexuality* Foucault isolated the "hysterization" of women's bodies and the socialization of procreative behavior as two key domains in which disciplinary technologies should be analyzed. Perhaps as an advocate of the "specific intellectual" he would have thought it best to leave specifically feminist research to those engaged in feminist struggle. In any case, he would have been the first to admit that one could do a genealogy of the genealogist. As an engaged critic, the genealogist does not transcend power relations. Indeed, the very idea of power-neutral theory is one that Foucault's own genealogies continually questioned.

Thus, I find it paradoxical that, in his essay "Disciplining Women: Michel Foucault and the Power of Feminist Discourse," Isaac Balbus stages a confrontation between Foucault and feminist mothering theorists in which he ultimately interprets Foucauldian genealogy as an example of the very type of emancipatory theory which it has consistently questioned. Assuming that, to a Foucauldian, mothering theory would look like a "paradigm case" of a "disciplinary true discourse," Balbus concludes that a Foucauldian feminism is a contradiction in terms.[4] In order to resolve this so-called contradiction, Balbus reformulates the Foucauldian position and presents us with two Foucaults, one who rejects mothering theory and another who is forced to concede that mothering theory is a liberatory discourse.

Balbus' argument for the latter rests on his uncovering a latent discourse within Foucault's writings in which Foucault implicitly appeals to categories that he manifestly rejects, namely, continuous history, the social totality, and a founding subject. According to Balbus, these categories are indispensable to feminist theory. Even more importantly, Balbus believes that for genealogy to be effective as social criticism, it must be grounded in an appeal to truth which is itself detached from the disciplinary power that it describes. If his discourse is not to be judged arbitrary and ineffective, argues Balbus, Foucault must exempt it from those forms of power/knowledge which it discloses. And once the

Foucauldian admits the distinction between emancipatory and authoritarian true discourse, he or she has no principled reason to reject the emancipatory claims of a psychoanalytic feminist theory.

My initial reaction to Balbus' essay was to ask: Do these two discourses really need to be reconciled? Would a Foucauldian reject mothering theory *tout court*? Are appeals to totality (whether historical or social), or to a continuous subject of history, indispensable to feminist theory? Must feminist theorists embrace the notion that all forms of patriarchy have maternal foundations? Clearly, the answer to the last question is "no." Many feminists have rejected psychoanalytic theory for non-Foucauldian reasons. More importantly, feminism is not monolithic but represents many different theoretical strategies.

Suppose, however, that we do identify feminism with its psychoanalytic versions. Would a Foucauldian then be committed to rejecting feminism? Again, I think not. Neither, apparently, does Balbus, but for different reasons. In his view, we must interpret Foucault either as an anti-feminist who, in his words, "disciplines women" by robbing them of the conceptual tools required in order to theorize and overcome male domination, or as an advocate of a humanistic feminism that as I shall argue, employs a juridico-discursive model of power and appeals to a quasi-biological, universal practice, namely, mothering as explanatorily basic.

In what follows I shall argue that Balbus presents us with a false alternative. We can slip between the horns of this dilemma by offering an interpretation of Foucault's genealogy which is neither inherently anti-feminist nor a masked version of the type of discourse it challenges. In the course of supplanting Balbus' paradoxical reading of Foucault, I shall also suggest the outlines of an alternative Foucauldian response to mothering theory which preserves the radical and innovative features of genealogy.

Genealogy: Grand Theory or Anti-Theory?

The principal targets of Foucault's genealogies of power/knowledge are the grand theories of society, history and politics which have emerged in the modern West. Most prominent among these, of course, are liberal humanism and Marxism (including its Freudian revisions). By "grand theory" I refer to any attempt to formulate a global or systematic discourse of the historical or social totality in order to legitimate programs and practices as progressive or emancipatory.

One of Foucault's more original moves involved isolating the similarities between two theoretical traditions that are more often contrasted. Thus, he claimed, both liberalism and Marxism operate with a juridico-discursive model of power consisting of the following basic assumptions: (1) power is possessed by a presocial individual, a class, a people; (2) power is centralized in the law, the economy, the State; and (3) power is primarily repressive. In his own analysis, Foucault represented power as exercised rather than possessed, as decentralized rather than exercised from the top down, and as productive rather than repressive. Equipped with this model of power, Foucault was able to focus on the power relations instead of the subjects related; to show how power relations at the microlevel of society make possible global effects of domination such as class or patriarchal power, without taking these theoretical unities as its starting point; and to give an account of how subjects are actually constituted through power relations. Foucault's model of power enabled him to trace the power effects of the theories themselves, power effects obscured by traditional theories of power.

Foucault adopted a skeptical stance toward the emancipatory claims of liberal and Marxist theories insofar as they were based on essentialist, total theories of humanity, its history, the economy, and libidinal economy.[5] His genealogy is not a theory of power or history in any traditional sense, but an anti-theory. Therefore, it does not tell us what is to be done or offer us a vision of a better society. Instead, the genealogist offers advice about how to look at established theories and a method for analyzing them in terms of power effects. Foucault's genealogies describe how some of our ways of thinking and doing have served to dominate us, how, in his words, "men (sic) govern themselves . . . through the production of truth."[6] They serve less to explain the real than to criticize other attempts to grasp it, particularly insofar as these attempts are reductionist, essentialist and presentist. Thus, it is misguided to turn to the genealogist for an endorsement of established theory.

When Balbus describes genealogy as an account of what power really is, when he suggests that Foucault offers a theory of history as a succession of power/knowledge regimes, and when he demands that Foucault accept his ahistorical criteria for distinguishing liberatory from authoritarian true discourses, he ignores Foucault's nominalism. "Power/knowledge" represents a grid of analysis, not a theory of power or history.[7] As such, Foucault's discourse on power does not attempt to displace others, but rather to get us to see them as material events with power effects.

If I am correct in maintaining that Foucauldian genealogy is not a theory, but an instrument for criticizing theories, then the basis for an alternative interpretation of the "latent" Foucault that Balbus uncovers is established. Balbus claims that a Foucauldian can endorse his own humanistic emancipatory theory once he or she recognizes the following: (1) that genealogy is implicitly committed to a distinction between libertarian and authoritarian true discourse; (2) that the totality envisioned by mothering theory is heterogeneous, not homogeneous; and (3) that the founding subject to which mothering theorists appeal is not the disembodied subject of liberalism which Foucault allegedly targeted, but an embodied subject.

In what follows I shall argue that Balbus' effort to reconcile Foucauldian and feminist discourse de-radicalizes Foucault's analysis of power and begs some of the most important questions that he raised.

Libertarian versus Authoritarian True Discourse?

Balbus argues that when Foucault attributes liberatory effects to his own critiques, he implicitly remains within the opposition between truth and power which genealogy opposes. Left without an appeal to truth free of power, genealogy remains groundless.

Here Balbus begs Foucault's question concerning the possibility of providing absolute foundations for any discourse. As David Hiley argues, genealogy need not appeal to a transhistorical ground to avoid the charge of arbitrariness, for the "alternative of 'either grounded or arbitrary' makes sense only within the framework Foucault's work has set aside."[8] Hiley continues:

> The sheer weight of detail and the force of his analysis support his abhorrence of modernity without having to have a meta-story to tell, and without grounding his interpretation. The charge of arbitrariness begs the question. The burden is on those who oppose his analysis to enter the dispute with a contrary vision, rather than pose the dilemma that Foucault must ground his inquiry or produce normative criteria. . . . Foucault could legitimately respond to questions about the correctness of his interpretation of the danger of normalization, not by producing criteria of correctness, but by shifting the burden of proof.[9]

Foucault resists establishing criteria for distinguishing libertarian from authoritarian discourse not because he believes that all true discourses are inevitably authoritarian (here Balbus has erected a straw figure), but because determining the liberatory status of any theoretical discourse is a matter of historical inquiry, not theoretical pronouncement. From a Foucauldian perspective, no discourse is inherently liberating or oppressive. This includes psychoanalytic discourses.

As evidence for this last claim, consider Foucault's observation that psychoanalysis played a liberating role in relation to psychiatry insofar as it denounced the complicity of psychiatrists with political regimes.[10] In a lecture from the same period, he suggested that psychoanalysis and Marxism have provided "useful tools for local research."[11]

Of course, Foucault also claimed that as a global theory psychoanalysis hindered research and contributed to forms of social control and normalization. But if we consider all of these statements in conjunction, we can only conclude that for Foucault, the status of psychoanalytic theory is ambiguous, a matter that must be judged by looking at specific instances, and not by setting up general criteria. No doubt this is the point Foucault was making in one of his last interviews when he said: "My point is not that everything is bad, but that everything is dangerous."[12]

So rather than seek to legitimate feminist psychoanalytic theory, a Foucauldian looks for its dangers, its normalizing tendencies. She asks how it might hinder research or serve as an instrument of domination despite the intentions of its creators. Whether it serves to dominate or to liberate is irrelevant to judging its truth. Foucauldian genealogy questions the idea that the only truth which is liberating is one which is free of power or untouched by history. Foucault borrows Nietzsche's hypothesis that power makes truth possible. Unlike Marxist ideology criticism, it does not relegate all knowledge claims conditioned by power to the domain of false consciousness. Indeed, Foucault did not question the truth of disciplinary knowledge as much as the particular ways in which it established the division between truth and falsity.[13] He described the historical conditions that made it possible for certain representations, objectifications and classifications of reality to dictate which kinds of statements come up as candidates for truth or falsity, which sorts of questions and answers were taken seriously. These conditions are not only constraining but also enabling. Presumably they contain possibilities for liberation as well as domination. As one commentator notes:

> If we cannot escape from history—and why should we hope to?—this does not entail confinement in prevailing political conditions, for history also includes the divisions and opposition that provide openness to the future.[14]

For example, the disciplinary knowledge brought to bear on the case of the hermaphrodite Herculine Barbin, whose memoirs Foucault unearthed and edited, is criticized not because it is untrue, but because it demanded that she be classified as either male or female and wrenched her from the "happy limbo" of ambiguous sexual identity.[15] It is not the truths about her as much as her being looked at through a particular mode of knowledge, a particular "regime of truth," which seals her fate. As Judith Butler states: "it is not her anatomy, but the ways in which that anatomy is 'invested' that causes the problem."[16]

What Balbus fails to take seriously is the way that genealogy suspends the identification of power and repression. Foucault rejects the view that liberatory knowledge is only possible where power relations are suspended. He observes: "Where there is power there is resistance; and yet, or rather consequently, this resistance is never in a position of exteriority in relation to power."[17] Thus, Foucault notes that the knowledge that constituted the homosexual as a particular type of individual made possible both medical and legal forms of social control over homosexuality as well as a form of resistance in which homosexuals embrace their identities and demand a right to their sexuality. The sword of knowledge is double-edged.

In other words, power relations are established within a historical field of conflict and struggle which contains within it possibilities of liberation and domination. Foucault denies that his own discourse is free of power relations without despairing about the possibility that it can have a liberatory effect. This is not liberation as transcendence of power or as global transformation, but rather freeing ourselves from the assumption that prevailing ways of understanding ourselves and others, and of theorizing the conditions for liberation, are necessary, self-evident and without effects of power.

The Question of Totality

As Balbus points out, Foucault criticized the concept of totality. His emphasis on discontinuity in history was motivated by a skepticism of total histories that represent the historical process as linear, cumulative and progressive. Nevertheless, in rejecting teleological histories of progress, Foucault was not rejecting the concept of continuity altogether. After all, genealogy involves reconstructing generative processes as well as locating discontinuities. Of course, the processes that he described are neither necessary, nor inevitably progressive.

Balbus incorrectly assumes that the purpose of genealogy is to *demonstrate* discontinuity. To the contrary, the isolation of discontinuities constitutes the starting point of genealogy, not its aim. For example, in *Discipline and Punish* Foucault locates a discontinuity between premodern and modern practices of punishment. He asks: How did imprisonment come to be accepted as the general form of punishment when it had been continually rejected by past penal reformers? Thus, isolating a discontinuity poses a historical problem. Foucault chose this particular problem because he questioned the value and function of our contemporary practice of imprisonment. He wanted to undercut our tendency to take imprisonment as a given by revealing its historical contingency.

Not only do continuist histories tend to legitimate rather than criticize present practices, they also obscure the conflicts and struggles in history. By pointing to paths that were not taken, unactualized possibilities and events that do not fit the functionalist schema of the total history, Foucault hoped to effect an "insurrection of subjugated knowledges."[18]

"Subjugated knowledges" refers not only to historical contents that are obscured within functionalist histories but also to those forms of experience that fall below the level of scientificity. The latter include the low-ranking knowledge of the psychiatric patient, the hysteric, the midwife, the housewife, and the mother, to name only a few. Because these disqualified knowledges arise out of the experience of oppression, resurrecting them serves a critical function. Through the retrieval of subjugated knowledge, one establishes a historical knowledge of resistance and struggle.

There is also the question of the social totality. Balbus takes *Discipline and Punish* to be a portrait of the whole of modern society as "disciplinary." Although this representation of Foucault's project is defensible—Foucault did resort to holistic rhetoric in this book—there are good reasons to reject it. First, one can argue that Foucault employed a holistic rhetoric of decline in order to counter the Whig historians' holistic rhetoric of progress. Second, Foucault's comments about the book indicate that it was not intended to be a portrait of the whole of society but, rather, a genealogy of the emergence of the ideal of a perfectly administered social system. Referring to his use of Bentham's Panopticon, Foucault remarks:

> If I had wanted to describe real "life" in the prisons, I wouldn't indeed have gone to Bentham. But the fact that real life isn't the same as theoretical schemas doesn't entail that these schemas are therefore utopian, imaginary, etc. That would be to have a very impoverished notion of the real.[19]

Bentham's Panopticon is not a metaphor for modern society, but an event, a fragment of reality, that Foucault analyzes in terms of its effects.

Contra Balbus, Foucault is not a holist but a particularist. He does not assume that all parts of society are systematically related. Instead, he begins with a particular practice in the present, the assumed value of which he is skeptical, and traces its lines of descent in Nietzschean fashion. These histories sometimes read like Spenglerian histories of decline because the point in the present toward which they lead is where Foucault locates a malevolent technology of power.

Given this account of Foucault's skepticism concerning the category of totality, we are in a position to evaluate Balbus' claim that the Foucauldian would accept the appeal of mothering theory to a heterogeneous social whole. This question of totality brings us to the heart of Balbus' critique of Foucault, and from a Foucauldian standpoint, to a major difficulty with mothering theory as Balbus characterizes it.

According to Balbus, appeals to continuous history and the social totality are indispensable to feminist theory, since it must be able to name the "massive continuity of male domination" which has persisted throughout changes in social and political formations, and which has pervaded all hitherto existing societies. Mothering theory provides an explanation of the origins of patriarchy which accounts for its depth and pervasiveness. Balbus says: "History has a meaning, and that meaning is the flight from and the repudiation of the mother."[20] This "flight" is allegedly caused by the universal practice of mother-monopolized child rearing. Thus, a necessary condition for the elimination of male domination (and the instrumental mode of rationality associated with it) is co-parenting, Balbus concludes:

> So it is that co-parenting is essential not only to overcome male domination but to supercede political and technological domination as well. It is in this sense that the struggle against patriarchy must be understood as a struggle for an entirely new civilization, a civilization without domination.[21]

Balbus' use of mothering theory involves many features of traditional emancipatory theories that Foucault criticized. He construes history as a a struggle between two groups, locates the origins of male domination within a key institution (mothering) which he takes as explanatorily basic, and on the basis of this reductionist explanation, prescribes and legitimates a particular progressive intervention, namely, co-parenting. Balbus says:

> Co-parenting is the key that can unlock the possibility of a society in which the nurturance and caring that have thus far been largely restricted in the arena of the family come to inform the entire field of human interaction.[22]

When Balbus argues that a Foucauldian could and should accept mothering theory as an emancipatory discourse because it appeals to non-developmental continuous history and a heterogeneous totality, he misses the point of Foucault's genealogy. It is not the empirical claim that male domination has appeared in many (even all) societies, the naming of patriarchy, which a Foucauldian would resist, but the attempt to deduce it from a general theory and to privilege a single locus of resistance. For a Foucauldian, patriarchy is the name of a global effect of domination made possible by a myriad of power relations at the microlevel of society. By eschewing reductionism, the Foucauldian can bring to light the heterogeneous forms that gender embodiment, the practice of mothering, and power relations producing gendered individuals take. Without rejecting mothering theory, the genealogist adopts a critical attitude toward it, specifically, toward the totalistic reductionism that obscures historical contents.

How might a Foucauldian respond to the tactics and categories of mothering theory? First, rather than assume that "mothering" represents a unitary phenomenon, the genealogist looks for discontinuities between practices and ideologies, and between practices across cultures. The inquiry might be sparked by numerous questions such as the following: When did the idea of the mother as an emotional nurturer emerge? When did the idea of women's status as reproducer prevail?

As Jean Grimshaw observes in *Philosophy and Feminist Thinking*, the idea of women as emotional nurturers of men was foreign to the Greeks.[23] Another feminist, Ruth Bleir, refers to cross-cultural comparisons that question the idea that "there is such a simple entity as 'women's status' throughout history."[24] "Women's work" and "men's work" have varied significantly in different societies. Bleir cites Karen Sacks' appeal to anthropological data which suggest that in some societies women's productive activities and social relationships condition the relations of reproduction. For example, !Kung women, nomadic gatherers who inhabit the Kalahari desert, nurse their babies for three years in order to control the spacing between births and thereby schedule childbearing to fit the demands of their productive activities. The contrary view of reproduction as explanatorily basic to understanding women's position, Bleir argues, "employs a fundamental assumption of biological determinist theories and reflects our own ethnocentric blindness to alternate modes of interpretation."[25] Finally, Foucault's histories of the rise of the life administering "biopower" suggest that the idea that exploring one's feelings is a key to the good life has emerged only recently, and its emergence has been linked to new mechanisms of social control. Thus, a Foucauldian might criticize mothering theory for its failure to adopt a historical attitude toward the value of feeling, nurturance, and caring. After all, Foucault described his project as a "genealogy of modern morals."

In effect, Balbus' tendency to identify mother-monopolized child rearing as a monolithic and fundamentally invariant phenomenon turns it into a quasi-biological given. The genealogical impulse is to inquire into the conditions of its genesis in order to reveal its historical limits. Despite pretensions to value heterogeneity, mothering theory obscures historical contents and experiential differences related to class, race, ethnic and other cultural variants. Balbus rightly values a heterogeneous society, but has not attended to the methodological prerequisites for bringing diversity to light.

Balbus' reference to a society without domination raises another point of contention between him and Foucault. For Foucault discourses were radical in terms of their effects, not their promises, or their claims to get at the root of a phenomenon. As I have argued, when viewed in terms of probable effects, mothering theory turns out to obscure more differences than it promotes. Moreover, a Foucauldian would resist Balbus' appeal to a power-free society. Balbus operates with the repressive hypothesis inasmuch as he claims that the power of the mother under mother-monopolized child rearing functions to repress the femininity of men (their relational capacities), and the masculinity of women (their capacity for autonomy). His assertion that lifting this power through co-parenting will lead to an authentic, integrated humanity represents theoretical humanism with a vengeance.

In contrast, the Foucauldian would look for the productive power of mothering theory, the normalizing tendencies as well as other possibilities that it creates in the social field. For example, as some feminists have already observed, mothering theory may unwittingly reinforce heterosexist norms. Moreover, Balbus himself admits (contra Chodorow) that "the commitment of mothering theorists to 'embodied identity' *perforce* entails a commitment to a specifically gendered identity."[26] It is clear that he has only two genders in mind. Yet, as Judith Butler points out, Foucauldian discourse challenges the assumption that sexual difference is irreducible when it rejects the idea that "sex" is either primary or univocal. The materiality of the body is significant only insofar as it is invested in historically specific ways.[27] Thus, mothering theory may enforce the restriction of gender to a binary division insofar as it assumes that bodily identity is determining.[28]

Finally, the model of liberation as total to which Balbus adheres is incompatible with the Foucauldian understanding of freedom and resistance. Foucault does not hope to transcend power relations altogether but rather to multiply the forms of resistance to the many forms that power relations take. To do this we must first bring the myriad forms into focus by utilizing the productive model of power. Thus, the Foucauldian tries to open up more space for resistance and self-creation by combatting the constraining effects of totalistic theories and the juridico-discursive model of power with which they operate.

What makes mothering theory problematic is not its endorsement of co-parenting, a worthy aim in itself, but rather its attempt to privilege and legitimate co-parenting on the basis of a quasi-essentialist science of gender. This tactic is objectionable because it ignores the many other rationalities within which appeals to the notion of a deep gender identity are found, as well as the myriad relations of power through which gender, and the "mother," are constituted.

The Subject of Foucauldian Feminism

This brings us to the question of identity. Postmodern feminists Nancy Fraser and Linda Nicholson have criticized mothering theory for adopting the Freudian premise "that there is a basic sense of self constituted at an early age through the child's interaction with its parents," and for assuming that this gendered deep self continues through adult life and cuts across divisions of race, class, ethnicity, and so forth.[29] A Foucauldian would reject the concept of a deep self for the same reasons that he or she rejects an ahistorical appeal to the theoretical category of mothering. It obscures cultural and historical specificity. Furthermore, inasmuch as mothering theory identifies male domination with a psychologically based male gender identity, it overlooks the complexities of institutional mediation which are surely also a part of the story of male domination. In contrast, a Foucauldian feminist would stress the sheer variety of ways in which effects of male domination are produced and gendered identities constituted.

That Balbus' feminist discourse refers to a material, embodied subject is not sufficient for it to escape the homogenizing theoretical tendencies that the Foucauldian abhors, as I have already argued above. Left without an appeal to an embodied founding subject, must the Foucauldian be left without any creative subjects whatsoever? To assume it must is to fail to take seriously Foucault's reasons for rejecting humanism. Indeed, Foucault does suspend the use of humanistic assumptions in order to account for how individuals are produced by disciplinary technologies. He believes that humanist discourses that place the subject at the center of reality or history have failed to grasp the extent to which the subject is fragmented and decentered in the social field. But to describe the ways in which individuals have been dominated through a rigid attachment to particular modern identities is not equivalent to rejecting identity *tout court*. As Ian Hacking notes: "Foucault said that the concept of Man is a fraud, not that you and I are nothing."[30] To suggest, as Foucault does, that the human is a social and historical construct is not to discredit every attempt to understand ourselves, but merely those that claim to be universal and to represent the Archimedean leverage point from which society might be moved.

Moreover, what Foucault objects to about psychoanalytic theories of identity is their tendency to represent individual identity as a fixed and unified phenomenon. Ironically, like mothering theorists, Foucault employs a relational model of identity. Rather than privilege any particular relationship as central to identity formation—for example, mother-infant relations—he highlights the many relationships through which individuals are produced. Thus, the Foucauldian need not exclude mothering theory altogether, but simply denies it theoretical privilege.

When Foucault speaks of power producing individuals, he refers not only to the production of individualist rhetoric, as Balbus suggests he does, but also to the production of forms of embodiment, of disciplined bodies. Foucault makes detailed and extensive references to the many techniques such as daily regimens and time-tables, methods for distributing and organizing bodies in space, drills, training exercises, examination and surveillance techniques, and so on. In effect, both the soul and the body are produced through disciplinary technologies.

Inspired by Foucault's descriptions of the ways in which modern individuals are produced, Sandra Bartky provides her own compelling descriptions of the disciplinary technologies that produce specifically feminine forms of embodiment, for example, dietary and fitness regimens, expert advice on how to walk, talk, dress, style one's hair, and wear one's make up. Bartky uses Foucault's model of power to show how these technologies subjugate by developing competencies, not simply by taking power away. She explains that one reason such technologies are so effective is that they involve the acquisition of skills, and are associated with a central component of feminine identity, namely, sexuality. The disciplines enhance the power of the subject while simultaneously subjugating her. Hence, women become attached to them and regard feminist critiques of the feminine aesthetic as a threat.

Nevertheless, Bartky also recognizes the ambiguity of these technologies. They produce possibilities of resistance as well. For example, new images of women are created when some women develop strong, muscular bodies. And as female body builders defy the canons of the feminine aesthetic, building their bodies beyond traditional limits, they destabilize feminine bodily identity and confuse gender.

Again, "where there is power, there is resistance." The Foucauldian does not view the relationship between the social and the individual as one of univocal determination, but as one of conflict and ambiguity. Individuals are the vehicles as well as the targets of power—a point which Balbus leaves out in his account of Foucault. In Foucault's relational view of identity, identity is fragmented and shifting. Black, lesbian, feminist, mother and poet, Audre Lorde, captures this conflict within the individual when she remarks: "I find I am constantly being encouraged to pluck out some one aspect of myself and present this as the meaningful whole, eclipsing other parts of self."[31] Eschewing the notion of a core identity, the genealogist attempts to mobilize the many sources of resistance made possible by the many ways in which individuals are constituted.

Stripped of its global dimensions, mothering theory might serve as an instrument of resistance to male-centered psychoanalytic theory. Mothering theory could be included as one among a plurality of tactics of resistance to male domination, but it would not be accorded the theoretical privilege which Balbus demands.

Conclusion

In claiming as he does that Foucault robs feminists of conceptual tools that are indispensable to feminist criticism, Balbus begs the most significant questions raised by Foucault's work, namely, questions concerning the nature of radical theory and practice. Foucault consistently questions the value of global theory, the idea of a power-free society, and the idea of a universal subject of history. As I have shown, Balbus' feminist discourse combines all three ideas. To argue that Foucault implicitly endorses this form of emancipatory theory is to fail to appreciate the limited but nevertheless radical nature of Foucault's project.

Foucault's project is limited because it is not a theory of society, history, or power in any traditional sense, but instead a suggestion about how to look at our theories. Foucault asks us to inquire into the effects of power which theories produce. Foucauldian discourse is radical not because it gets at the roots of domination, but inasmuch as it introduces radically new questions and problems concerning prevailing ways of understanding ourselves which continue to dominate our thinking about radical social transformation. Foucault does not offer an alternative emancipatory theory but, rather, tools that might free us from an unquestioning adherence to established ways of thinking. Ultimately, the radical nature of Foucault's discourse, like any other, must be judged on the basis of the effects that it produces.

I have argued that Foucauldian discourse might serve as an effective instrument of criticism for feminists who have experienced the oppressive dimensions of claims to know based on the authority of male-dominated sciences; the inhibiting effects of radical social theories that privilege one form of oppression over another and thereby devalue feminist struggle; and the multiplicity of subtle forms of social control which are found in the micro-practices of daily life. In exposing the distortions in Balbus' treatment of Foucault, I hope to have paved the way for an alternative rapprochement between Foucault and feminist discourse which does not require that we abandon either of them.

To the question whether a Foucauldian feminism is a contradiction in terms, a Foucauldian feminist might reply; "No, not a contradiction but a continual contestation." Any self-critical and historically inflected feminism will find Foucauldian genealogy indispensable.[32]

4

Disciplining Mothers: Feminism and the New Reproductive Technologies

Although he intended to, Foucault never wrote a history of women's bodies. Yet, had he proceeded according to his original plan, he would have written a volume in the *History of Sexuality* entitled *Woman, Mother and Hysteric*. It was to be a study of the sexualization of women's bodies and of concepts of pathology related to it such as hysteria, neurasthenia, and frigidity. Foucault intended to locate the processes through which women's bodies were controlled through a set of discourses and practices governing both the individual's body and the health, education and welfare of the population, namely, the discourses and practices of "biopower."[1]

In contrast to the often sporadic, violent power over a relatively anonymous social body exercised under older, monarchical forms of power, biopower emerges as an apparently benevolent, but peculiarly invasive and effective form of social control. It evolved in two basic and inter-related forms. One of these, disciplinary power, is a knowledge of and power over the individual body—its capacities, gestures, movements, location, and behaviors. Disciplinary practices represent the body as a machine. They aim to render the individual both more powerful, productive, useful *and* docile. They are located within institutions such as hospitals, schools, and prisons, but also at the microlevel of society in the everyday activities and habits of individuals. They secure their hold not through the threat of violence or force, but rather by creating desires, attaching individuals to specific identities, and establishing norms against which individuals and their behaviors and bodies are judged and against which they police themselves.

The other form of biopower is a regulatory power inscribed in policies and interventions governing the population. This so-called "biopolitics of the population" is focused on the "species body," the body that serves as the basis of biological processes affecting birth, death, the level of health and longevity. It is the target of state interventions and the object of study in demography, public health agencies, health economics and so forth.

If, as Foucault claimed, biopower was an indispensable element in the development of capitalism insofar as it made possible a "controlled insertion of bodies into the machinery of production," then it must also have been indispensable to patriarchal power insofar as it provided instruments for the insertion of women's bodies into the machinery of reproduction.[2] And if claiming a right to one's body only makes sense against the background of these new life-administering forms of power and knowledge, then the history of modern feminist struggles for reproductive freedom is a key dimension of the history of biopower.

Of course, Foucault abandoned the project of writing a history of women's bodies. In many of his later writings, the absence of specific attention to women's sexual and procreative bodies as pivotal targets for the new forms of power that he described is glaring. Given Foucault's belief that it is best to facilitate ways for the oppressed to speak for themselves, it is perhaps fitting that the task of writing these histories has been left to feminists. And feminists have been writing them. Barbara Ehrenreich, Deirdre English, Adrienne Rich, Mary Daly, Linda Gordon, Gena Corea, Rosalind Petchesky, Rita Arditti, Ruth Hubbard, to name only a few, have all contributed to the development of feminist analyses of reproductive politics. [3]

The most recent chapter in the feminist history of biopower addresses the social and political implications of the emergence of new reproductive technologies, namely, in vitro fertilization and other test tube techniques, as well as antenatal testing procedures such as amniocentesis, ultrasound and genetic screening. Although feminist analyses of these technologies are by no means unified, it is in the writings of Gena Corea and other members of the Feminist International Network on Resistance to Reproductive and Genetic Engineering (FINRRAGE) that we find the most influential and provocative critiques. Corea and her colleagues have uncovered crucial information about the development and implementation of new reproductive technologies. Their writings have increased scientific and technological literacy among feminists, a much needed service. They place women at the center of their analyses calling our attention to the risks these technologies pose to women—physically, psychologically and politically.

After reading Corea's *The Mother Machine*, I was convinced that the introduction of new reproductive technologies does pose real dangers to women.[4] Yet, I was also troubled by Corea's analysis and its implications for feminist reproductive politics, for there are real disadvantages to the assumptions about power and subjectivity that inform it. Insofar as her approach has become a model, it is important to address it critically.[5]

In what follows I provide the outlines of a Foucauldian feminist analysis of the new reproductive technologies in order to highlight its advantages over prevailing radical feminist critiques. I begin by providing a reading of the radical feminist critiques. I consider their understanding of "technology", their account of the origins of new reproductive technologies in the history of modern medical practice, their diagnoses of the dangers they pose to women and, finally, their strategies of resistance. I shall also address the theories of power and subjectivity that ground their analyses. Then I turn to my own Foucauldian analysis of both the radical feminist discourses about the technologies and the technologies themselves. My purpose here is not to discredit FINRRAGE, for I believe that it has played a crucial role in politicizing new reproductive technologies. FINRRAGE has succeeded in creating collective agencies focused on bringing the uses and abuses of these technologies to the attention of an international feminist public. It has established its own and provoked other oppositional discourses that can be further developed and used to resist their dangerous implications.

However, much of this oppositional discourse is too pessimistic, moralistic and one-dimensional. Corea and other radical feminists demonize the technologies and the men who design and implement them. They focus almost excusively on the dominant discourses and practices governing reproduction and therefore pay insufficient attention to the resistance and struggle that is already taking place in the context of reproductive politics. Their anti-technology stance sometimes lapses into utopian romantic appeals to a pre-modern era and is therefore not helpful to the majority of women facing decisions about childbirth in the United States today. More adequate analyses would make clearer why many women regard them as beneficial. They would also highlight the different positions that women occupy in relation to the new technologies in order to identify multiple sites of potential resistance.

In the final analysis, the Foucauldian feminist and radical feminist positions will, no doubt, overlap; for both assume that new reproductive technologies pose dangers for women. Both also regard them as potentially insidious forms of social control. I will argue, however, that the disciplinary model of power and its corresponding view of the subject provide a better framework for criticism and for identifying possibilities of effective resistance. The types of resistance called forth by this model enlist the support of women located at a variety of different social sites—as upper middle class recipients of infertility services, as poor women with insufficent access to adequate prenatal care, or as feminist activists working within and outside the boundaries of existing health care institutions to transform them.

My efforts to offer an alternative analysis of the dangers of the new reproductive technologies that relies heavily on Foucault's notion of disciplinary power is not without its ironies. On the one hand, as I have already indicated, Foucault's own histories of political technologies of the body fail to address their gendered character. Despite this fact, feminists have used his insights to develop a specifically feminist analysis of disciplinary technologies investing women's bodies. Also, many have criticized Foucault's description of the rise of biopower as too dystopian and pessimistic. To such critics it represents a one-dimensional containment of modern humanity reminiscent of a Weberian iron cage or Herbert Marcuse's "technological rationality." Thus, he too has been accused of paying insufficient attention to non-hegemonic discourses and practices of resistance.

As I have already argued elsewhere, although Foucault did sometimes write as though the hold of disciplinary power was total, to interpret his histories of power's intersection with knowledge as Whig histories in reverse is to overlook his claim that resistance and struggle are co-present with power and that power is continually transformed in the face of such resistance.[6] Whereas Foucault's *Discipline and Punish* did focus primarily on the power of expert and institutionalized discourses, in *The History of Sexuality* he began to emphasize resistance. Furthermore, some feminists who have turned to his critical discourse for their own analyses have further developed the notion of the resistant subject implicit in the later writings.[7]

Mother Machines: Technology as Male Domination

As I have indicated, Gena Corea's *The Mother Machine* is perhaps the most influential and paradigmatic of feminist critiques of new reproductive technologies. It is a polemical and pessimistic analysis involving a dystopian projection of a world in which women's bodies are reduced to medically manipulable objects, to the living laboratories of male "technodocs" bent on appropriating the last source of power left to women—the procreative power of motherhood. As her title suggests, Corea believes that the ultimate aim of the new reproductive technologies is to replace biological mothers with "mother machines" by supplementing already existing test-tube fertilization techniques (for instance, in vitro fertilization, embryo replacement, embryo transfer, embryo freezing) with frontier technologies such as artificial wombs and cloning. She laments the fragmentation of the once unified biological process of motherhood into separate functions—that is, egg donor, womb donor, and social mother—as a dangerous degradation of motherhood. As these separate functions are increasingly controlled and regulated by male-dominated medical, legal and governmental agencies, and as the rights of fetuses begin to override those of the mother, Corea fears that women's appeals to reproduction as a basis of power will be totally eroded. According to Corea, the new technologies fragment and commodify women's procreative bodies in a process analogous to the one perpetrated on their sexual bodies. She envisions a high-tech version of the "reproductive brothel" (a term she borrows from Andrea Dworkin) portrayed in Margaret Atwood's *The Handmaid's Tail*. In this scenario women are explicitly reduced to the functions of servicing men as childbearers, domestic servants, childrearers, and mistresses.

In many respects, the analysis of Corea and other FINRRAGE activists is convincing. They point out that infertility clinics present experimental in vitro fertilization procedures with low success rates (20 percent at best) as though they are therapies despite the fact that many of the expensive, hence not widely accessible, technologies have not been extensively tested for the risks they pose to the women undergoing them at their own expense. Moreover, they argue that the tendency to treat infertility as an individual medical problem effectively depoliticizes it and deflects attention from other potential causes of infertility such as environmental pollution, work hazards, smoking and iatrogenically produced conditions. In addition, there are disturbing eugenic implications of genetic counselling made possible by antenatal testing procedures. Decision-making that takes place in response to information from these tests constructs new norms of fetal quality and threatens to lead to a situation where the choice to refuse antenatal testing or to abort a potentially disabled fetus is lost. Some feminists fear that the choice of in-body fertilization and, eventually, in-body pregnancy may be lost as well owing to the tendency of medicine to regard women's bodies as dangerous and diseased and its own interventions as beneficial.[8]

Overall, Corea and others maintain that the new "choices" that these technologies offer to women are illusory. The discourse of increased options and less risky birthing practices serves to cover up an underlying process in which women's options are increasingly controlled by male experts. They ask whether a woman's choice to undergo the emotionally and physically grueling procedures for infertility treatment can possibly be voluntary. Women are portrayed either as innocent and ignorant victims of the medical establishment or as unwitting colluders in a horrifying extension of patriarchal control over women's bodies. In short, women's consciousness is reduced to false consciousness.

Ostensibly, the view of technology that grounds much of the radical feminist discussion of new reproductive technologies is the view that technology is neither inherently liberating nor repressive, but rather neutral. Its meaning derives from the social and political context in which it is embedded. Nevertheless, for the most part, radicals describe the relationship between patriarchal technologies and domination as total. In effect, patriarchal modes of thinking and behaving, and the technological instruments of patriarchy, become inherently dominating, controlling, and objectifying.[9] In this latest phase of the history of male domination, domination perpetuates itself as technology.

Indeed, any adequate feminist analysis of the new reproductive technologies must consider the patriarchal contexts in which they are embedded. But the crucial question for assessing their implications for women is how one characterizes "patriarchy." What are its origins? What are its primary means of exercising power? Who are its principle agents? Depending upon how one answers such questions, one's assessment of the dangers of these new technologies and the best strategies of resisting them will vary.

The "Origins" of New Reproductive Technologies: A Radical Feminist Account

In order to highlight the advantages of a Foucauldian feminist technology criticism over the prevailing radical feminist version, it is useful to contrast their respective stories of the origins of these technologies. Corea and other radical feminists give both psychological and historical accounts. On the one hand, they represent new reproductive technologies as the quintessential embodiment of a "male reality" that is violent, objectifying, controlling, dehumanizing, denaturing, flesh-loathing and misogynist. They depict high technology childbirth practices as the instruments through which men will finally satisfy an unconscious desire to procreate and thereby to eliminate their dependency on women. They represent them as the final steps of a continuous historical process of increasing control over women's bodies which aims to appropriate the power associated with procreation and, ultimately, to eliminate the need for women altogether.

Feminist object relations theories of masculinity support this psychological reading of the origins of the male dominated medical model of pregnancy and childbirth. They link typical masculine traits to characteristics valued in science such as detached objectivity, autonomy, separation, and an aggressive and controlling stance toward nature. For example, Evelyn Fox Keller provides a psychoanalytic interpretation of the writings of Francis Bacon, an early spokesman for the view that the aim of science is to control nature, in order to illustrate the gendered nature of the modern scientific enterprise.[10] Bacon uses sexual and gendered imagery to describe the relationship between mind and nature. Nature is depicted as the bride of mind whose task is to seduce, shape, subdue and conquer "her".[11] At first glance, it would seem that the scientific mind is wholly masculine. Nevertheless, Keller finds in Bacon's image of scientific mind a repressed feminine element, that is, an acknowledgement of the necessity for the scientist to be receptive and creative. Whereas Bacon reserved the procreative function for God, the modern scientist arrogates the procreative function to himself in a "simultaneous appropriation and denial of the feminine."[12] Thus, according to Keller, at its psychological and historical origins, modern science exhibits the desire to appropriate and control the feminine both within itself and in its metaphorical extension, nature.[13]

Radical feminists offer historical accounts of the development of modern obstetrical practice that reverse the narratives of linear progress provided by many traditional historians.[14] Traditional historians describe the development of modern obstetrics as a process wherein childbirth was removed from a female realm of ignorance and superstition to the enlightened realm of male physicians with the scientific knowledge and technical skills needed to rescue women from the risks and pain of childbirth. Traditional medical scholars focus on the history of the growth of scientific and clinical knowledge with little emphasis on the practice of medicine. In contrast, feminists describe the "medicalization" of childbirth as the transformation of pregnancy into a disease and the takeover of a female-centered natural process attended by skilled and caring midwives by a group of male physicians interested in establishing and expanding their practices, their occupational status and authority, *and* their control over women.[15]

Before the late eighteenth century, the primary role of the physician was to intervene in problem childbirths in order to save either the mother or infant. Birth was primarily a female affair and a social or family, not a medical event. Attracted by the new obstetricians' promises of safer, less painful labor, women—particularly urban, middle-, and upper-class women—increasingly began to turn to physicians during the nineteenth century. However, evidence suggests that childbirth was just as risky under the care of nineteenth-century obstetricians as it had been without them. In the United States at this time, practitioners were not likely to be well trained or up-to-date on the latest developments in the physiology of labor, anesthesiology or gynecological surgery despite the fact that these developments are often pointed to by medical scholars to attest to the competence of early obstetricians.

Physicians were predisposed toward heroic interventions with forceps, drugs and other questionable techniques. Hence, from the beginning, modern medicine attracted clients through technological innovation. Although most births still took place in the home, those who were sent to hospitals, usually poorer urban women, faced the risk of childbed fever because the use of antiseptics was not routine until the end of the century. In exchange for their services, physicians used poor urban women as a resource for medical teaching.

It was not until the twentieth century that American physicians consolidated their control. In the first decade of this century, physicians waged a successful campaign against midwives, scapegoating them for the high maternal death rate. Between 1920 and 1960 the percentage of at home births dropped from 75 percent to 4 percent. Childbirth was handled as a surgical procedure. During this period of increasing medical control over childbirth, a "normal" delivery was likely to involve forceps, unnecessary surgical intervention, drugs to induce labor and reduce the pain of labor, and the lithotomy position. It was also common to separate mother and child at birth and to discourage breastfeeding. Indeed, maternal and infant mortality rates actually increased after midwives were eliminated.

Radical feminist interpretations of these events portray them as part of a continuous and teleological process wherein patriarchal medicine monopolizes control over women's procreative bodies and reduces women to passive objects of medical surveillance and management. They claim that childbirth was less risky before this medical takeover. They argue that the new reproductive technologies are distinct from other forms of patriarchal control insofar as they shift the locus of male control from sexuality to reproduction, that is, from individual men in the context of the family to medical experts who derive their authority from science. Nevertheless, although the men are different, the techniques are portrayed as remarkably similar. Medical interventions such as the introduction of forceps, the routine use of drug induced labor, anasthesia, twilight sleep, caesarian sections, and more recently, new reproductive technologies are not hailed as progressive, but rather are depicted as violent and invasive distortions of the natural birthing process. Images of dying women, women with leeches on their cervixes, or with pelvises crushed by the indiscriminate use of forceps, of drugged women, women strapped to birthing tables, or constrained by fetal monitors attached to their bodies pervade the radical feminist accounts of the history of obstetrics. The new reproductive technologies, particularly test tube techniques and genetic engineering, are described as the latest and, allegedly, most deadly development in this history of the medical takeover of women's bodies. In effect, medical practices are regarded as continuous with other practices of violence against women such as genital mutililation, foot binding, and battering.

Corea maintains that if medical scientists succeed in perfecting frontier technologies such as artifical wombs, then women will no longer be needed. She suggests that the implications may ultimately be gynocidal. And if the development of such techniques does not lead to gynocide, Jalna Hamner warns, they will indeed threaten to make women's experience of reproduction as discontinuous as that of men.[16] The physicians who manage high technology childbirth may even come to identify with fetuses more than women do. Moreover, Hamner fears that insofar as these techniques sever reproduction from women's biological bodies, a connection that some feminists regard as a source of power and that is clearly a source of our identities as women, they may lead to increased alienation—a loss of self.

What does FINRRAGE recommend that we do about these technologies? Among the resolutions made at a 1985 FINRRAGE conference in Vallinge, Sweden are the following:

> We want to maintain the integrity and embodiment of women's procreativity. . . . The division, fragmentation, and separation of the female body into distinct parts for its scientific recombination disrupts historical continuity and identity.

> We call for all women to resist the take-over of our bodies for male use, for profit making, population control, medical experimentation and misogynous science.

> We seek a different kind of science and technology that respects the dignity of womankind and of all life on earth. We call upon women and men to break the fatal link between mechanistic science and vested industrial interests and to take part with us in the development of a new unity of knowledge and life.[17]

In short, FINRRAGE calls for a halt to further development and use of in vitro techniques. They ask feminists to fight the privatization and isolation of motherhood through consciousness-raising and further education. Other suggestions include setting up an international tribunal of medical crimes against women or setting up a monitoring agency on the model of the Environmental Protection Agency.[18] Finally, they recommend that women resist the hegemony of the Western medical model of pregnancy and childbirth by separating or withdrawing from it altogether. In other words, they encourage us to expand feminist self-help and home-birth movements in the absence of a liberated science and technology.

In appealing to a more organic model of pregnancy and childbirth, radical feminist critiques of new reproductive technologies build on the writings of feminists such as Carolyn Merchant, who, in *The Death of Nature*, isolates the salient connections between capitalist interests in the domination and disenchantment of nature and patriarchal discourses that identify women with nature.[19] She suggests that changing conceptions of nature, for instance the shift from the premodern model of nature as an organism with its own inviolable integrity to the modern philosophy of nature as a machine, can be linked both to the emergence of capitalism and to new strategies of patriarchal power. By the seventeenth century, the mechanical philosophy of nature succeeded in reducing the natural realm (hence, the body) to machine-like entities that require repair and intervention by scientific experts. Stripped of its organic, nurturant and animistic qualities, nature appeared as a resource for unlimited human use and control. In other words, nature ceased to pose a limit to the scope of human behavior and became instead an object of scientific investigation. Thus, the new mechanistic philosophy of nature served both capitalist and patriarchal interests insofar as it opened up new territories (the earth, women's bodies) for exploration and exploitation.

The view that science and technology aim to dominate nature is of course fairly common among non-feminist critics of science as well. Merchant's analysis serves as a feminist corrective to the gender-blind tradition of technology criticism found in the writings of members of the Frankfurt School. Max Horkheimer, Theodor Adorno, Herbert Marcuse and Jurgen Habermas offer powerful analyses of how class domination has been served by the growth of technology, but fail to address its implications for gender politics.

In particular, Marcuse's *One Dimensional Man* provides an analysis of modern technology as a form of social control and domination that is remarkably similar to the radical feminist treatments of new reproductive technologies. He described the increasing rationalization and bureacratization of everyday life, the commodification of human relations, and the monopolization of power by professional elites brought about under industrial capitalism with the development of modern science and technology. He introduces the concept of "technological rationality," a form of rationality with totalitarian implications that depoliticizes social relations by reducing moral and political questions to technical ones. In a controversial move, he equated modern science and technology with domination: "Today, domination perpetuates and extends itself not only through technology but as technology."[20] He called for a "feminine" alternative in which the scientist would assume a more responsive, receptive and nurturant relationship to nature in a liberated social context: "[T]here are two kinds of mastery: a repressive and a liberating one."[21]

Marcuse's tendency in *One Dimensional Man* to describe the relationship between modern science and technology and domination as total, and his utopian appeal to a new, "feminized" science and technology, overlap significantly with radical feminist strategies. Foucault's analysis of disciplinary power overlaps to some degree with that of Marcuse. But his analysis was also developed as an alternative to Critical Theory. Foucault criticized Marcuse for giving repression (of sexuality, of the body) an exaggerated role in his account of modern capitalist forms of social control. He also rejected the view that the connection between class dominance (and by extension, gender dominance) and technological production is total. Insofar as feminist critiques of the new reproductive technologies construe the relationship between domination, technology and subjectivity in ways that overlap with Critical Theorists, Foucault's analysis is useful in developing a response to them.

What would a Foucauldian feminist critique of the new reproductive technologies look like? How would it account for their origins? How would it differ from the thesis of technology as male domination represented in radical feminist discourses? What strategies of resistance would it propose?

The "Origins " of New Reproductive Technologies: A Foucauldian Account

Told from a Foucauldian perspective, the history of women's procreative bodies is a history with multiple origins, that is, a history of multiple centers of power, multiple innovations, with no discrete or unified origin. It is a history marked by resistance and struggle. Thinking specifically about the history of childbirth in America, a Foucauldian feminist does not assume a priori that the new reproductive technologies are the product of a long standing male "desire" to control women's bodies or to usurp procreation. This does not mean that such motives do not play a role in this history of medicalization, but it does deny that they direct the historical process overall.[22]

Foucault described the social field as a network of intersecting practices and discourses, an interplay of non-egalitarian, shifting power relations. Individuals and groups do not possess power but rather occupy various and shifting positions in this network of relations—positions of power and resistance. Thus, although policies governing reproductive medicine and new reproductive technologies in the United States today are indeed largely controlled by non-feminist and anti-feminist forces, it is plausible to assume that women and feminists have played a role in defining past and current practices, for better or worse. It is also the case that these non- and anti-feminist forces are not unified or monolithic. Their control is neither total nor centrally orchestrated.

Employing a bottom-up analysis, a Foucauldian feminist would describe the present situation as the outcome of a myriad of micro-practices, struggles, tactics and counter-tactics among such agencies. Consequently, in describing the history of childbirth practices, she would focus not only on the dominant discourses and practices, namely, those of medical experts and the so-called "technodocs," but also on the moments of resistance that have resulted in transforming these practices over the years.[23] Indeed, there are many discourses and practices in the contexts of medicine, law, religion, family planning agencies, consumer protection agencies, the insurance and pharmaceutical industries, the women's health movement, and social welfare agencies that struggle to influence reproductive politics and the social construction of motherhood. As Paula Treichler states:

> The position of modern medicine was not monolithic but emerged gradually in the course of key debates, federal initiatives, strains between private practitioners and academic physicians, and debates within medicine over what its professional hierarchy was to be . . . Physicians did not uniformly declare a war on nature, nor decide that they should adopt an ideology of intervention and subordination.[24]

Medicalized childbirth has come under attack from many camps since the birth of modern medicine. Individual men and women as well as organized groups representing scientific, economic and feminist interests have consistently challenged the Western medical model of childbirth. In the second half of this century there have been continual demands for alternatives to the medical model of childbirth. For example, after World War II, Grantly Read, a British obstetrician criticized physicians for ignoring women's subjective experience of childbirth and for interfering with the natural birthing process. Lamaze was introduced and became increasingly popular. Natural childbirth was reintroduced as an option and a home-birth movement emerged. La Leche League encouraged women to disregard medical advice that favored bottle feeding and encouraged them to return to breastfeeding. In addition, there were proposals to admit fathers into delivery rooms, to eradicate the routine use of the lithotomy position, and to stop separating mothers and babies at birth. Both feminists and non-feminist critics have challenged the routine use of episiotomy, and of drugs for pain and the induction of labor. Furthermore, individual women attempt to control the terms of their own hospital childbirths by staying home longer before going into the hospital and thereby avoiding unnecessary C-sections due to prolonged labor, by demanding that they have an advocate present during the birthing process, by finding physicians who support their desire to minimize medical intervention, and so forth. Such resistance has served as the basis of forms of client resistance and has worked to counter tendencies toward depoliticizing motherhood and childbirth.

Highlighting the struggles surrounding the definition of childbirth and motherhood does not suggest that medicine has not had a monopoly over childbirth during this century, but rather that this control was not simply imposed from the top down. It had to be won and continually faces resistance. Nor do I mean to imply that challenges to medicine such as those advocating "natural" childbirth have not been coopted to some extent. After all, sometimes resistance is wholly neutralized by the counter strategies of the hegemonic, white, upper middle-class, heterosexual scientific and medical establishments. For example, many natural childbirth classes offered in hospitals continue to train women to expect and accept medical interventions such as fetal monitors, intravenous drugs, labor induction, forceps, pain medication, and even Caeserian sections.[25] The ideology of the "natural" has been used in the service of both feminist and antifeminist struggles. Regardless, identifying such struggles undercuts assumptions that the medical control of childbirth is one-dimensional or total.

Disciplining Mothers

As I have indicated, Foucault identified the history of women's bodies as a key dimension of the history of biopower. Understood as part of this history, new reproductive technologies represent the most recent of a set of discourses (systems of knowledge, classification, measurement, testing, treatment and so forth) that constitute a disciplinary technology of sex that was developed and implemented by the bourgeoisie at the end of the eighteenth century as a means of consolidating its power, improving itself, "maximizing life." Disciplinary technologies are not primarily repressive mechanisms. In other words, they do not operate primarily through violence against or seizure of women's bodies or bodily processes, but rather by producing new objects and subjects of knowledge, by inciting and channeling desires, generating and focusing individual and group energies, and establishing bodily norms and techniques for observing, monitoring, and controlling bodily movements, processes, and capacities. Disciplinary technologies control the body through techniques that simultaneously render it more useful, more powerful and more docile.

New reproductive technologies represent one of a series of types of body management that have emerged over the past two decades rendering women's bodies more mobilizable in the service of changing utilities of dominant agencies.[26] Their aim is less to eliminate the need for women than to make their bodies even more useful. They enhance the utility of women's bodies for multiple shifting needs. As Linda Singer aptly noted:

> The well managed body of the 80s is constructed so as to be even more multifunctional than its predecessors. It is a body that can be used for wage, labor, sex, reproduction, mothering, spectacle, exercise, or even invisibility, as the situation demands.[27]

Singer points out that fertility technologies can be used either for purposes of consolidating race and class privilege or for eliminating competition in the labor market from white, upper middle-class women who have delayed pregnancy for careers.

New reproductive technologies clearly fit the model of disciplinary power. They involve sophisticated techniques of surveillance and examination (for instance, ultrasound, fetal monitors, amniocentisis, antenatal testing procedures) that make both female bodies and fetuses visible to anonymous agents in ways that facilitate the creation of new objects and subjects of medical as well as legal and state intervention. Among the individuals created by these new technologies are infertile, surrogate and genetically impaired mothers, mothers whose bodies are not fit for pregnancy (either biologically or socially), mothers who are psychologically unfit for fertility treatments, mothers whose wombs are hostile environments to fetuses, mothers who are deemed "negligent" for not choosing to undergo tests, abort genetically "deficient" fetuses, or consent to caesarian sections. As these medical disciplines isolate specific types of abnormality or deviancy, they contruct new norms of healthy and responsible motherhood. Additionally, insofar as the new technologies locate the problem of infertility within individuals, they deflect attention and energy that could be used to address the environmental causes of infertility. Hence, they tend to depoliticize infertility. They link up with the logic of consumerism and commodification by inciting the desire for "better babies" and by creating a market in reproductive body parts, namely, eggs, wombs, and embryos. Finally, they make women's bodies useful to agencies that regulate and coordinate populations.

At the same time that these new technologies create new subjects—that is, fit mothers, unfit mothers, infertile women, and so forth—they create the possibility of new sites of resistance. Lesbians and single women can challenge these norms by demanding access to infertility treatments. Women who have undergone infertility treatment can share their experiences and demand improvements or expose inadequacies in the model of treatment. The question is not whether these women are victims of false consciousness insofar as they desire to be biological mothers, as much as it is one of devising feminist strategies in struggles over who defines women's needs and how they are satisfied.

To suggest that the new reproductive technologies "produce" problems and desires and thereby contribute to the further medicalization of mothers' bodies is not to suggest that these problems (for instance, infertility) are not real, that the experts are charlatans, and that those who seek their advice are blinded by the ideology of medical science. It does not imply that things were better before these technologies appeared. It does suggest, however, that part of the attraction of the new technologies is that many women perceive them as enabling. Of course, referring to them as disciplinary technologies does highlight their controlling functions. Yet, this control is not secured primarily through violence or coercion, but rather by producing new norms of motherhood, by attaching women to their identities as mothers, and by offering women specific kinds of solutions to problems they face. In fact, there may be better solutions; and there may be better ways of defining the problems. There is the danger that medical solutions will become the only ones and that other ways of defining them will be eclipsed.

This emphasis on normalization as opposed to violence represents a major advantage of the disciplinary model of power. If patriarchal power operated primarily through violence, objectification and repression, why would women subject themselves to it willingly? On the other hand, if it also operates by inciting desire, attaching individuals to specific identities, and addressing real needs, then it is easier to understand how it has been so effective at getting a grip on us.

Moreover, although the model of patriarchy as violence against women is appropriate in many contexts, I question its use in the context of critiques of medicine. Are all forms of objectification, even those that involve inequalities of power, inevitably violent? While many forms of surgical intervention are experienced as traumatic, are they best described as a form of "violence against the body"? Emily Martin has written that Foucault was wrong to claim that the violent tactics of juridical or monarchical power have been replaced by the more subtle tactics of disciplinary power. She states: "dismemberment is with us still, and the 'hold on the body' has not so much slackened as it has moved from the law to science."[28] Without suggesting that there have not been many incidences of unjust or callous use of power over women in medical contexts, it is important to avoid reducing all of Western medical science and technology to another example of violence against women. Many of its practices are clearly distinct from sadistic or coercive violence. At the very least the rhetoric of violence is likely to be politically ineffective since it does not resonate with so many of the women who must rely on medical institutions for health care.

This is only one of several political disadvantages of the repressive model of power with which radical feminists have operated. Another related difficulty is that it employs a binary model of alternatives, either repressive technology or a liberatory one, either a masculinist science or a feminist one, either mechanistic materialism or naturalism, either a technological approach or a natural one. This politically and cognitively restrictive binary logic stems in part from the tendency to portray patriarchal power in monolithic, essentialist and totalistic terms. It is limiting because it detemporalizes the process of social change by conceiving of it as a negation of the present rather than as emerging from possibilities in the present. In so doing, it restricts our political imaginations and keeps us from looking for the ambiguities, contradictions and liberatory possibilities in the technological tranformations of conception, pregnancy and childbirth.

The repressive model of power assumes that all women and men occupy essentially the same position in relation to patriarchy, namely, that of victims who are blinded by the ideology of science or perpetrators of violence, respectively. Like the discourses and practices they criticize, radical feminist discourses often position women as passive subjects not potential activists, as causally conditioned not self-determining, as morally or politically corrupted. Thus, they fail to take some women's expressed "needs" (for fertility treatment, for genetic screening) seriously.[29] They provide inadequate explanations of how some women's interests appear to be bound up with the system of male domination. They also ignore the fact that some men, even physicians, are potential allies in struggles against domination.

In contrast, there are significant political advantages to adopting Foucault's disciplinary model of power for a feminist critique of new reproductive technologies. Operating with a model of the social field as a field of struggle consisting of multiple centers of power confronting multiple centers of resistance prompts us to look for the diverse relationships that women occupy in relation to these technologies, and for the many intersecting subject positions constituting the social field. We become focused on the pregnant or infertile woman in all of her social relationships, not simply her relationship to the physician. She may be a working woman, a welfare mother, a woman of color, a drug addict, a physician, a lawyer, a feminist. By directing our attention to the differences among women and to the intersecting social relations in which women are situated, we are more likely to locate the conflicting meanings and contradictions associated with the technological transformation of pregnancy.

Although it is crucial to continue to identify the ways in which new reproductive technologies threaten to erode women's power over their reproductive lives, it is also important to locate the potential for resistance in the current social field, that is, what Foucault refers to as "subjugated knowledges"—forms of experience and knowledge that "have been disqualified as inadequate ... or insufficiently elaborated: naive knowledges, located low down in the hierarchy beneath the required level of cognition or scientificity."[30] This means looking not only at the discourses of the men who develop and implement the technologies, but also at the different ways in which women are being affected by them, that is, the material conditions of their lives, their own descriptions of their needs, and of their experiences of pregnancy and childbirth. Not all women have equal access to the most advanced medical technologies. For the majority of women, withdrawal from medical institutions is not an option. Indeed, inadequate access to health care and to information is the key issue for a majority of women in the United States today.

Despite her rejection of Foucault's position on violence, Emily Martin provides an example of such an approach in her book *The Woman in the Body*. She explores differences between middle-class and working-class women's experiences of pregnancy and childbirth and juxtaposes them with dominant mechanistic scientific and medical accounts of these same processes. She concludes that the dominant ideology is partial, that middle-class women are more inclined toward the medical view of themselves, and that working-class women described their experiences more in terms of non-medical aspects of their lives. She suggests that there is liberatory potential in resurrecting these subjugated discourses of bodily experience—that they might serve as critical feminist standpoints on medical discourse and practice.

Martin's observations are consistent with those of Rayna Rapp in her writings on amniocentesis and genetic counseling.[31] Rapp observes that the group best served by advances in reproductive medicine—white middle-class women—are also the most vulnerable to its powerful definitions of motherhood. This is the group of women who are most likely to become agents of fetal quality control. In her studies, Rapp found that the interpretations given of positive test results for Down's syndrome varies with differences in class, race or ethnicity. For example, to a Hispanic woman in the urban ghetto whose "normal" children confront serious obstacles to self-actualization, the meaning of being "disabled" may be different. She may be more likely to opt to have a disabled child than her white middle-class counterpart.

Thus, although new reproductive technologies certainly threaten to reproduce and enhance existing power relations, they also introduce new possibilities for disruption and resistance.[32] Using Foucault's model of power as a shifting and unstable set of relations, and his understanding of discourses as ambiguous and polyvalent, we are encouraged to look for such possibilities in the present and to mobilize them as a means of challenging hegemonic reproductive relations on a variety of political fronts. As reproductive issues are increasingly taken up as cultural, not simply biological issues, more space is opened up for politicizing them. For example, Rapp suggests that the idea of quality control of fetuses can be used to support demands for adequate prenatal care for all women. And, ultimately, as these technologies desta-bilize current conceptions of motherhood, opportunities for identifying and legitimating alternative forms of motherhood are presented.

"Motherhood" and "technology" are highly contested concepts in contemporary America. As an identity, an ideology and an institution, motherhood has been both a source of power and enslavement for women. But it is important for feminists not to assume that any one aspect of female practice is central to patriarchal control. We must not conflate motherhood and femininity, or motherhood and childbirth. Motherhood has biological meanings, but also many social ones. In arguing that new reproductive technologies may lead to the elimination of women altogether, Corea and others ignore the many, often conflicting, roles and positions that women occupy in contemporary society, the many services they provide, the many other ways in which their bodies are disciplined as mothers, workers, housewives, sexual beings, and so forth. Sandra Bartky suggests that normative femininity—a set of disciplinary practices regulating the body, its gestures, appetite, shape, size, movement, appearance and so forth—has come to center more on sexuality and appearance than on the maternal body.[33] Whether this is the case or not, it highlights the fact that women's bodies have many uses. Feminists must resist those forces that aim to enlist such practices in the service of docility and gender normalization and struggle to define them differently. But this is not tantamount to rejecting them entirely.

Similarly, there are many possibilities for a technological transformation of pregnancy that might benefit women. Of course, we cannot overlook the fact that scientific and technological practices are largely controlled by men. Nevertheless, there are good reasons to avoid reducing patriarchal domination to its technologies. As history reveals, technological developments are many edged. Who, in retrospect, would deny women many of the contraceptive technologies that were developed and introduced in this century? Both feminists and anti-feminists resisted the legalization of birth control. Feminists saw birth control as a means for men to escape their responsibility to women. Anti-feminists feared that if women had more control over their biological reproductive processes, they would reject their social roles as mothers and wives. (Like some radical feminists today, they tended to conflate control over the biological process of motherhood with control over motherhood itself.) As Linda Gordon points out, birth control has been a progressive development for women only to the extent that the women's movement has continually struggled to define policies regulating their development and use.[34] But rather than reject newly emerging technologies outright, feminists can meet multiple-edged developments with multiple-edged responses. We can resist the dangerous trends, the tendencies toward depoliticization, privatization, decreased autonomy, and the elision of women's experiences and interests in the process of developing and implementing reproductive technologies and the laws and policies regulating them. We can also allow ourselves to envision utopian possibilities for technologically transforming reproduction.[35]

Finally, at the same time that people in developed countries embrace new technologies with little resistance, there is also evidence in film, literature and the media of increasing cultural anxiety about the pace of technological change. The prospects of nuclear accidents or nuclear warfare loom large in the collective psyche. This ambivalence about technology can be tapped in efforts to democratize the process of technological innovation, design and implementation.

In an intriguing essay, Donna Haraway argues that images of the cyborg, of couplings between organism and machine, provide an imaginative resource for contemporary feminist politics.[36] Without either wholly natural or technological origins, cyborgs

> are not afraid of their joint kinship with animals and machines, not afraid of permanently partial identities and contradictory standpoints. The political struggle is to see from both perspectives at once because each reveals both dominations and possibilities unimaginable from the other vantage point.[37]

Similarly, Foucault's understanding of power as decentralized, as a myriad of shifting relations, enables us to avoid the extremes of dystopian or utopian political critique in favor of locating many positive and negative political and strategic possibilities presented in the present. From a Foucauldian perspective, every strategy or counter-strategy is potentially dangerous. Appeals to a more holistic, unified,"natural", "maternal," or "feminine" experience of childbirth become merely one of several strategies that we might deploy in efforts to resist the medical takeover of women's bodies. In themselves, they are no less cooptable than high technology approaches. Indeed, holism and naturalism can and have been used for patriarchal as well as feminist ends.

De-medicalization is also not sufficient as a strategy for resisting the hegemonic forces that govern our bodies under patriarchal capitalism. De-medicalizing childbirth does remove it from this authoritarian context and open up more possibilities for contesting its meaning. Nevertheless, as Paula Treichler notes, de-medicalization also brings risks. It places childbirth in the public sphere where it "can more easily be represented as a commodity, not only in the economic marketplace but in the ideological and social marketplace as well."[38] Moreover, an open marketplace provides opportunities for exploitation and abuse. After all, infertility, pregnancy, and childbirth *are* partly medical issues. Rather than remove them from medical control, we can support efforts to build health care institutions that enable women and those whom they love to structure childbearing around their own needs. This will surely include expanding access to a variety of reproductive services that are currently made available only to privileged women, but will also require that we question current uses and modes of implementation.

What makes new reproductive technologies especially dangerous to women is not so much that they objectify and fragment bodily processes, but that they are designed and implemented by experts in contexts where scientific and medical authority is wielded with insufficient attention to the prerequisites for democratic or shared decision-making. The often unchallenged authority of experts makes possible an imposition of treatments and regimes that is in fact dangerous to women. Physicians and health care practictioners must be exhorted to further efforts to ensure that women are not treated solely as bodies, but also as subjects with desires, fears, special needs, and so forth. Of course, as I have attempted to show, many of the new reproductive techologies do operate through modes of "subjectification," that is, by classifying and identifying subjects in efforts to further control them. So, attending to subjectivity is not a sufficient condition for ensuring that the pernicious effects of Western models of medicine are combatted. But it is necessary if individuals are to have more control over how their medical needs are satisfied. The authority of Western medicine has been challenged increasingly during the past three decades. Memories of thalidomide babies and the scandal of DES can be redeployed. Many individuals and groups resist medical authority and treatment everyday, for better or worse. Such resistance can be mobilized in efforts to eradicate the non-reciprocal relations of power so often still characteristic of the physician-patient relationship.

As I have already suggested, feminists are not the only ones resisting developments in reproductive medicine. We can also coalesce with other movements challenging current forms of organization and authority within health care institutions. We can build political unities not on the basis of some naturalized identity as women, or mothers, but on the basis of common political opposition and affinities with other political struggles. We can also continue to make demands for equal access to health care, for better information, and for more democratic processes of developing, designing, implementing and regulating new technologies.

Analyses that simply reject new reproductive technologies do not assist women in making choices. Nor do they lead to creative political strategies. We must provide analyses that enable women to assess risks and benefits—both individual and social, and that facilitate feminist and other oppositional struggles that are already ongoing in the context of health care institutions. We must provide analyses that bolster feminist political struggles for economic resources, information, acccss to health care, shared decision-making. We must build alliances across race, class, sexual differences and differences in ability.

On the basis of the Foucauldian analysis suggested here, one might conclude that some of the budding biotechnological developments should be resisted altogether at the present time. Up to this point I have treated new reproductive technologies as a whole, primarily for the sake of a more general metatheoretical analysis. Still, any adequate feminist analysis of new reproductive technologies must treat them separately. Of course, one must also pay attention to the ways in which they overlap and reinforce one another. Use of one technology often leads to or even requires use of another. Accordingly, if one opts for in vitro fertilization, one is also likely undergo the whole range of antenatal testing procedures as well as caesarian section. But this does not mean that each of the procedures carries the same dangers or offers the same possibilities to women. We may ultimately want to preserve some and eliminate others.

In vitro fertilization is especially suspect. Success rates are exceedingly low, the procedures are physically and psychologically grueling, and the health risks they pose to women have not been adequately measured. Most importantly, because in vitro techniques require significant expertise and are very expensive, much of the control over how they are implemented and who is eligible to receive them is monopolized by the scientists, technicians and administrators who offer them. At present, in vitro fertilization is available primarily to married, white, upper middle-class women who perceive biological motherhood as very desirable and who convince practitioners that they desire a child enough to withstand the treatment. The criteria for eligibility reinforce a traditional classist, racist, and heterosexist ideology of fit motherhood. Moreover, these women have little control over the process once they agree to undergo treatment. Finally, given that in vitro fertilization could be described as a failure due to such low success rates, we might ask what function this failure is serving. Scientists interested in research on human embryos have a vested interest in promoting the benefits of in vitro fertilization partly because the techniques employed yield "surplus" embryos. As I am writing this, there is pressure on Congress to lift the ban on human embryo research. In short, there are reasons to believe that in vitro clinics are not really serving women at all.

But, in general, our conclusions about the value of these technologies will be reached on the basis of a different analysis—one that is more inclusive, pluralistic, and complex, one that looks for their ambiguous implications and identifies the many agencies struggling to define motherhood and childbirth in contemporary America in an effort to mobilize oppositional forces. New reproductive technologies clearly threaten to make women's procreative bodies more effective targets for the intervention of hegemonic patriarchal and capitalist forces in contemporary America. As disciplinary technologies they represent a potentially insidious form of social control since they operate by inciting the desires of those who seek them out. But the question whether these techniques also offer more liberatory possibilities will depend on the extent to which mechanisms for resisting their pernicious disciplinary implications are devised. Feminist efforts to identify strategies of resistance will be aided by analyses that move beyond moralism, or nostalgia for a more female-centered era of "natural" childbirth, and begin to look for the complex connections between the power/knowledge relations of biopower and other factors influencing sexual struggle. I have argued that a Foucauldian feminist approach is more likely to produce such analyses.[39]

5

Foucault and Feminism:
A Critical Reappraisal

Feminist appropriations of Foucault have resulted in path-breaking and provocative social and cultural criticism. Original analyses of anorexia nervosa, the social construction of feminin-ity, female sexual desire, sexual liberation, the politics of needs and the politics of differences have changed the landscape of feminist theory.[1] Why has Foucault's poststructuralist discourse been of special interest to feminists? Foucault's attention to the productive nature of power, and his emphasis on the body as a target and vehicle of modern disciplinary practices were compati-ble with already developing feminist insights about the politics of personal life, the ambiguous nature of the so-called "sexual revolution" in the sixties, the power of internalized oppression, and the seeming intractability of gender as a key to personal identity. In addition, Foucault was one of the most politically engaged of the poststructuralists. He did not confine his political interventions to the experiments in playing with language char-acteristic of the literary avant-garde. His books were intended to serve as interventions in contemporary practices that govern the lives of oppressed groups such as homosexuals, mental pa-tients and prisoners. Moreover, his skeptical attitude toward Enlightenment humanism, universalist histories and traditional emancipatory theories coincided with feminist critiques of the limits of liberalism and Marxism.[2]

Recently, however, some feminists have put the feminist collaboration with Foucault into question. They argue that feminist appropriations of Foucault's discourses on subjectivity, power and resistance threaten to undermine the emancipatory project of feminism. In a provocative essay Linda Alcoff claims that Foucault's descriptions of Enlightenment humanism and the constitution of the modern subject as key dimensions of the rise of disciplinary forms of "subjection" deprive feminism of any effective agency or sense of authority.[3] His politics of self-refusal allegedly leaves feminism with no standpoint from which to engage in an emancipatory politics and nothing to strive for. Alcoff also criticizes Foucault for appealing to micro-politics without providing any analysis of the overall structures of domination. Thus, she argues, he provides neither a theory of resistance nor a basis for judging between subjugated forms of experience that are truly resistant to hegemonic power relations and those which are not. According to Alcoff, Foucault leaves feminism with no normative or theoretical basis for making political judgments.[4]

In a similar vein, both Barbara Christian and Nancy Hartsock raise suspicions about Foucault's poststructuralist critiques of subjectivity and humanism.[5] They argue that its influence and prevalence overshadows the efforts of third-world and minority cultures to establish their own identities and literatures as oppositional to the hegemonic forces of patriarchal and imperialist capitalism. In general, these critiques portray poststructuralist discourses as too relativistic, nihilistic and pessimistic to serve as a basis for an adequate feminist politics.

My initial reaction to such criticisms in the past has been to defend Foucault, for I think they either beg important questions about humanism and liberatory politics raised by Foucault's discourses, or misunderstand the nature of his project. After all, an ironic tension permeated Foucault's discourse. He refused the role of visionary, but introduced his genealogies of modern power/knowledge in order to free up the possibilities for new forms of life. He undermined Enlightenment humanism in order to prepare the way for new forms of experience. He was a pessimist committed to political activism. That he has been labelled structural determinist and voluntarist, activist and fatalist, leftist and neoconservative suggests either that his own discourse was incoherent and confused or that his interpreters have been unwilling to suspend traditional assumptions and categories when judging it.

I think both alternatives are partially correct. On the one hand, Foucault was famous for shifting direction and abandoning the project of developing ideas laid out in earlier books. Many diverse interpretations of Foucault's "position" can and have been defended with reference to his texts and interviews. His later work on the ethics of the self could be read as an effort to re-engage in a dialogue with humanism. On the other hand, many of these interpretations beg the questions that Foucault raises. Are there not good historical reasons to be suspicious of universalist history, or the search for anthropological foundations and master schemes for social transformation? Doesn't the rise of new social movements in the United States and Western Europe put into question the binary models that privilege the struggles between proletarian and bourgeois capitalist, or men and women, as primary within an emancipatory politics? Haven't the interiorization of humanity and processes of individualization (for instance, the creation of the homosexual, hysteric or criminal personality) been linked to pernicious forms of social control? Is there not good reason to be wary of the constitution of theoretical unities such as "women's experience," "lesbian experience," and "the third world" insofar as they inevitably suppress important differences?

There may also be good reasons for continuing to operate with many of the categories and assumptions of traditional revolutionary theory. Nevertheless, Foucault has opened the question from a perspective that is sympathetic with demands for radical change. He does so by writing histories that focus our attention on how traditional emancipatory theories and strategies have been blind to their own dominating tendencies. He suggests that they are historically linked to disciplinary practices that have been more oppressive than liberating.

While I clearly believe there is much of value for feminism in Foucault and that the answer to many of the questions posed above is yes, any feminist appropriation of the "male-stream" tradition must be critical. In my own work, I have reconstructed a version of Foucault that I find useful for addressing issues in American feminist theory and practice. Sometimes this has meant emphasizing aspects of his discourse that he did not develop sufficiently, and de-emphasizing others. For instance, I have continually stressed and attempted to develop his remarks about resistance and struggle found in later interviews and in *The History of Sexuality* and de-emphasized or dismissed the totalistic rhetoric of decline found in *Discipline and Punish*. Moreover, as Foucault himself urged, one must look for the effects of power produced by all discursive practices, including his own. So, there are indeed limits to the feminist collaboration with Foucault. Some of these limits are due to the limited nature of Foucault's project itself. Others are the consequence of his androcentrism. In what follows, I shall address both.

Foucault's Critical Project

Much criticism of Foucault stems from a lack of clarity about the nature of his project. His own remarks about the trajectory of his work often contributed to this lack of clarity. Was he actually developing a "theory" of power, or of resistance at all? Foucault was less a political theorist than a historian engaged in metatheoretical critique. Nevertheless, his critique of humanism and disciplinary power did imply that traditional categories and assumptions informing modern practices, particularly therapeutic and other liberatory practices rooted in certain understandings of identity, are dangerous. His genealogy of modern power/knowledge did challenge political orientations that presuppose that power is primarily repressive. His emphasis on power relations at the microlevel of society did suggest that state-centered and economistic political strategies do not capture power where it is most effective. And insofar as the micro-practices of power that he described constitute a shared background of habits and dispositions that are rarely questioned and in fact not really chosen in any conscious sense, he implied that much of history is beyond our control. For Foucault, the heritage of cultural and political traditions and the range of choices we have for defining ourselves and our political perspectives are themselves not chosen. Genealogy was his method for investigating the historical origins of some of this heritage and for resisting it insofar as it is linked with domination.

One could argue that it is politically irresponsible to radically question existing theoretical and political options without taking any responsibility for the impact that such critique will have and without offering any alternative. Insofar as Foucault identified impersonal forces and tendencies in history beyond the direct control of individual and collective agents, he did confront a dilemma. If much of history is beyond control, then what sense does it make to resist at all? Aren't his own "political" interventions left without any coherence or justification insofar as they seem to presuppose the very norms and values that he puts into question?

One strategy for slipping between the horns of this dilemma is to suggest that Foucault's contributions consist primarily of attempting to bring to our awareness the deep regularities and broad and impersonal forces that make us what we are, that define our sense of alternatives and what it makes sense to do in certain contexts in order to free us from them. In other words, while he may have denied that much of what informs our modern sensibility was not chosen, this does not mean that one cannot attempt to bring to light the anonymous historical processes through which this sensibility was constituted in an effort to create a critical distance on it. According to Foucault, our freedom consists in our ability to transform our relationship to tradition and not in being able to control the direction that the future will take.[6]

How does he justify his protests? There are two alternatives. He can deny that protest against oppression requires any neutral standpoint of justification at all. The fact is that people often **do** resist what they regard as oppressive circumstances. The specific categories and practices that Foucault identifies as particularly dangerous—modern processes of individualization and normalization found in the discourses and institutions of psychiatry, sociology, criminology and so forth—are those that he was motivated to resist based upon his own experiences. As a "homosexual author" Foucault was also a product of the disciplinary technologies that constituted modern notions of authority and sexual identity.[7] At the same time, he resisted them. One of his strategies of resistance was to describe the historical process through which sexual practices came to be identified as central to personality—for example, the process through which the homosexual identity was constituted. He believed that liberation struggles rooted in demands for a right to one's sexuality are limited insofar as they accept the fixing of sexual identity established by institutions interested in regulating and controlling it. He hoped to stimulate other avenues of resistance to the disciplinary technologies of sex in addition to those premised on embracing homosexuality as a natural fact—to open up possibilities for other ways of experiencing ourselves as sexual subjects. Thus, he resisted the idea of a fixed sexual identity at the same time that he believed, of course, that homosexuals should have civil liberties as homosexuals. In any case, Foucault's own protest is testimony to the fact that he did not believe that the normalizing processes that he described were total.[8] It is also evidence that he did not entirely reject the notion of agency. The fact that one cannot guarantee the outcome of such resistance is no argument against it. It is, instead, a reason to continue to be attentive to the limits of one's own discourses and practices.

In the absence of alternatives to present principles and values governing political struggle, we must continue to appeal to the standards of rationality and justice that are available to us within the specific contexts in which we find ourselves. These standards do not unilaterally determine one choice rather than another—how they are to be interpreted is itself a matter of struggle—but they do constitute a ground for critique and for justification. In other words, appeals to rights, liberties, and justice (and struggles over how to interpret these principles) are not denied to us.

These are the only sorts of appeals that make sense to us right now.[9]

Foucault did not often adopt the latter alternative. But neither does his discourse deny us this option.[10] His genealogies of modern power/knowledge were not designed to show that Enlightenment forms of rationality were inherently linked to practices of domination, only that some of them were historically linked. Thus, he leaves open the possibility of disarticulating Enlightenment ideals from such practices.[11]

Nevertheless, he preferred to operate at a different level— the metathcoretical level of the genealogist. He wrote histories that brought to light the dangers but also the contingent character of Enlightenment principles and categories. Thus, genealogy is both a justificatory and an emancipatory strategy. On the one hand, the stories that he tells are designed to justify his claims that certain practices are more enslaving than liberating. On the other hand, his genealogies are "histories of the present." In other words, Foucault wrote from the perspective of a future historian in order to defamiliarize present practices and categories, to make them seem less self-evident and necessary. He attempted to free a space for the invention of new forms of rationality and experience. But this does not necessarily invalidate the efforts of those who continue to struggle within the contraints of the old ones.[12]

As one commentator has aptly characterized it, "freedom" in Foucault's politics consisted of "a constant attempt at self-disengagement and self-invention."[13] We are free in being able to question and reevaluate our inherited identities and values, and to challenge received interpretations of them.

As feminists, I believe that we have good reason to appeal to Foucault's negative freedom, that is, the freedom to disengage from our political identities, our presumptions about gender differences, and the categories and practices that define feminism. We must cultivate this freedom because feminism has developed in the context of oppression. Women are produced by patriarchal power at the same time that they resist it. There are good reasons to be ambivalent about the liberatory possibilities of appealing to "reason," "motherhood," or the "feminine" when they have also been the source of our oppression. Even the recent history of feminism in the late twentieth century suggests that feminism has often been blind to the dominating tendencies of its own theories and to the broader social forces that undermine and redirect its agendas. Consequently, as I have argued elsewhere, genealogy is indispensable to feminism.[14]

I also believe that we need more than genealogical critique. Feminist practice must inevitably be negative and, I believe, skeptical. Yet, attempts to free ourselves from certain forms of experience and self-understanding inherited under conditions of domination and subordination are not enough. We must also continue to struggle for rights, justice and liberties within the constraints of modernity.[15] We must also continue to envision alternative future possibilities. If there is indeed anything in Foucault's philosophy that prevents us from doing this, then we should reject it. As I have argued, I do not believe that there is.

Foucault's Androcentrism

Analyzing the power relations governing the production and dissemination of discourses was, of course, one of Foucault's principal projects. His preoccupation with thinking against oneself, his reluctance to speak for others and to make political judgments were rooted in an aversion to authority and in his belief that intellectuals often over-extend the limits of whatever authority they do possess. He suspected every position of maintaining itself by suppressing differences and uncertainties. Moreover, he was sensitive to the fact that oppositional discourses often unwittingly extend the very relations of domination that they are resisting. He would have been the first to endorse a genealogy of the genealogist.

In what follows I shall address some of the effects of male privilege and androcentrism in Foucault's discourse. There are tendencies and emphases there which must, at the very least, be regarded as "risky" for feminism. I borrow this term from Ann Ferguson.[16] Risky practices are those about which there is conflicting evidence concerning their practical and political implications. There are good reasons to adopt them and good reasons to doubt them. In other words, calling practices risky implies that although there is no hard and fast evidence that they lead to or perpetuate relations of domination, there is also sufficient reason to question them.

Risk taking has always been a part of feminism. In fact, one could argue that feminism is always at risk. Appealing to post-structuralist discourses seems especially risky since they do challenge us to suspend traditional assumptions about liberation and power, particularly the assumption that we must establish foundations for our own discourses, without offering any alternative political theory. As I have suggested above, Foucault thought that suspending traditional assumptions was crucial for bringing about new ways of thinking and new forms of life. To the extent that he developed a politics, it was a politics of uncertainty. I think he believed that one must always feel uncomfortable with one's political principles and strategies lest they become dogma. Accordingly, he valorized critique over vision and the destabilization of identity over its formation. It is to this aspect of his thought that I want to turn since it is here that I have my own doubts about the use of Foucault for feminism.

Foucault was notorious for his critique of modern humanism. And, as I have indicated, feminist critics of Foucault find in this critique a wholesale rejection of subjectivity and agency. But to focus on the ways in which the subject is in fact constituted, and on the broader social and political forces that determine the parameters and possibililities of rational agency is not to deny agency. It does, however, point to its limits.

I understand Foucault's project itself as presupposing the existence of a critical subject, one capable of critical historical reflection, refusal and invention. This subject does not control the overall direction of history, but it is able to choose among the discourses and practices available to it and to use them creatively.[17] It is also able to reflect upon the implications of its choices as they are taken up and transformed in a hierarchical network of power relations. Finally, this subject can suspend adherence to certain principles and assumptions, or to specific interpretations of them, in efforts to invent new ones. Foucault's subject is neither entirely autonomous nor enslaved, neither the originator of the discourses and practices that constitute its experiences nor determined by them.[18]

This account of subjectivity is compatible with the insights underpinning the feminist practice of consciousness-raising. On the one hand, consciousness-raising assumes that our relationships to ourselves and to reality contain elements of domination that can lead to collaboration in our own oppression. On the other hand, it presupposes that the meaning of these experiences is not fixed, but rather subject to reinterpretation and collective critical analysis. In some models the aim of consciousness-raising is not the development of a unified feminist consciousness but rather a critical consciousness and a recognition of oppression.[19] In her classic essay on feminist consciousness raising Sandra Bartky describes the process as one that leads to awareness of oppression, victimization, category confusion and a sense of moral ambiguity.[20] Destabilization of identity is often the most profound effect of consciousness raising, not the creation of a unified sense of self.

Foucault's account of subjectivity does not introduce any obstacles to feminist praxis that were not already there. Feminist praxis is continually caught between appeals to a free subject and an awareness of victimization. Foucault suggests that this tension may be permanent, that both views are partially correct, and that living in this uncomfortable tension is an important catalyst for resistance and wariness.

But there are other dimensions of Foucault's discourses on subjectivity and resistance that are risky. As we have seen, he sometimes endorsed practices of self-erasure and self-refusal. Ironically, he gained notoriety for efforts to disavow his own authority. In his last writings he spoke increasingly of the need to think against oneself, one's identities and attachments. Confessional practices aiming at self-disclosure and self-discovery were questioned insofar as they are linked with disciplinary technologies of domination. Indeed, Foucault was suspicious of most efforts to tell the truth about oneself, for they often involve relations of power in which as "confessing subject" one is subject to the judgment of an expert administering needs for the state.

Of course, any radical theorist in the twentieth century must take seriously the morally and politically suspect implications of the emergence of bourgeois preoccupations with the self—with individuality and self-discovery—in the West and with therapeutic techniques for engaging in such self-discovery. Foucault's own stories of the disciplinary subjection of the modern individual through practices of identity formation, confession and self-improvement are convincing. Clearly, many aspects of feminine identity have been enslaving. Yet, Foucault's emphasis on the dangers of identity formation can all too easily become the basis for repudiating women's struggles to attain a sense of identity not defined by patriarchal interests. Indeed, one could argue that one of the conditions for the possibility of forming an oppositional women's movement is that women come to an awareness of themselves as *worth* fighting for.

Nancy Hartsock has asked: Why, at the point in history when feminist voices, authorities and identities are being established, do poststructuralist critiques of authority, identity and personal narratives become fashionable? Even more forcefully, Caren Kaplan asks: "Who dares to let go of their respective representations and systems of meaning, their identity politics and theoretical homes when it is . . . a matter of life and death?"[21] This characterization of the implications of poststructuralist critiques like that of Foucault may not be entirely accurate, for it speaks more to the "assimilation" and domestication of poststructuralism in the American academy than it does to many of the "original" discourses themselves. As poststructuralism has been assimilated, it has often been stripped of its more radical impulses. Poststructuralism, and what Barbara Christian refers to as the "race for theory," do threaten to overshadow and supplant the political literature and theories of women, people of color, third-world writers, and so forth.[22] After all, poststructuralist literary theory, for all of its potential, is an invention of disenchanted white males. It is not surprising that it should become more important than the subjugated discourses of the "other" about which it speaks.

While self-refusal may be an appropriate practice for a privileged white male intellectual such as Foucault, it is less obviously strategic for feminists and other disempowered groups. As women, many of us have been taught to efface ourselves as a matter of course. Someone has suggested that Anonymous was a woman. The absence of a sense of self, of one's value and authority, and of the legitimacy of one's needs and feelings is a hallmark of femininity as it has been defined in many patriarchal contexts. A principal aim of feminism has been to build women's self-esteem—the sense of confidence and identity necessary for developing an oppositional movement.[23]

Telling our stories to one another has been an important part of this process. It could even be argued that feminist psychotherapies that cultivate a certain self-proccupation and self-assertion have helped women to avoid the tendency to lose themselves in others, particularly men. Even more important are the practices of truth telling associated with breaking through the silence of the many women who have suffered the trauma and violence of sexual and physical abuse. Such experiences can lead to forms of self-dispersal, detachment and dissociation which are so debilitating as to prevent an individual from participating in anything but "pathological" forms of protest such as eating disorders, multiple personality disorders and the inability to form any intimate personal relationships at all. Feminist therapeutic practices designed to uncover this scandal and break the silence can indeed disrupt patriarchal power relations. Of course, as Adrienne Rich points out: "Breaking the silences, telling our tales, is not enough. We can value the process—and the courage it may require—without believing that it is an end in itself."[24] In order to be politically mobilized, this truth must be shared, collectively analyzed and strategically deployed in feminist political struggle.

Thus, the strategic value for feminism of building identities, whether through literature or feminist therapeutic practices, will depend upon the contexts in which it is done. Whose identity? To what end? Some women's voices are more authoritative than others. For example, my identity as a white feminist theorist in the academy may be more in need of destabilization than that of my black feminist counterpart. We must be prepared to ask ourselves: What is the price of the authority that we do attain? How is it constituted? To what extent does it require identifying ourselves with capitalist or patriarchal forces? Does it reproduce and legitimize patriarchal discourses and practices? Does it suppress other voices?

So too will the value of engaging in confessional practices be measured. To whom is one confessing? To what end? Some forms of self-preoccupation are more politically suspect than others. A retreat into oneself can represent an escape from political reality, or it can be a temporary strategy for getting clear about some of the conditions governing one's choices, and thereby free one up for new ways of thinking, new choices.

So, Foucault's emphasis on self-refusal and displacement could be risky insofar as it might undermine the self-assertion of oppositional groups and suppress the emergence of oppositional consciousness. At the same time, he rightly calls to our attention the risks involved in becoming too comfortable with oneself, one's community, one's sense of reality, one's "truths," the ground on which one's feminist consciousness emerges. Teresa de Lauretis has described feminist theory as requiring

> leaving or giving up a place that is safe, that is "home"—physically, emotionally, linguistically, epistemologically—for another place that is unknown and risky, that is not only emotionally but conceptually other; a place of discourse from which speaking and thinking are at best tentative, uncertain, unguaranteed.[25]

She suggests that this is not so much a choice as it is a necessary feature of feminism. There can be no "home", no completely secure place for women within the context of classist, racist and heterosexist patriarchal society. Leaving our homes is not a choice, she says, for "one could not live there in the first place."[26] From de Lauretis' point of view, a perspective that I find to be wholly compatible with and better developed than Foucault's account of resistant subjectivity, the feminist subject continually operates both from within and outside of traditions and communities. This "eccentric" perspective, as she refers to it, is necessary if feminism is to remain critical and to avoid premature and exclusive closure of its categories, communities and practices. De Lauretis suggests that it has been feminists of color and lesbian feminists—feminists often marginalized in mainstream feminism—who have been the first to recognize the fact that to be a feminist is to constantly put oneself at risk, to be dislocated, to have to remap the "boundaries between identities and communities."[27]

Clearly, it would be a mistake to jettison appeals to identity and confessional truth telling in slavish devotion to Foucault's skepticism. His discourses also bear the traces of his own social and historical location as a white male theorist. Although his homosexuality may have served to sensitize him to the experience of oppression and to the situations of marginal and oppressed groups, it did not prevent him from becoming a leading intellectual force. It is just as important to use Foucault against himself, and against the use of his work to undermine the very struggles he claimed to support, as it is to criticize dangerous tendencies within feminism. But it would also be a mistake to assume uncritically feminist political theories and practices developed in the context of patriarchal capitalism. A critical feminist theory has built into it a certain resistance to identification, or, as de Lauretis describes it, a "dis-identification with femininity" insofar as it has been male-defined.[28] In the final analysis, we have here another example of the double bind characteristic of every situation of oppression. Identity formation is both strategically necessary and dangerous. And, as feminists we must live within the tension and uncertainty produced by our oppressive situations.

Perhaps one of Foucault's most important insights is his insistence that one's theoretical imperatives and commitments be motivated by specific practical imperatives. He wrote from the perspective of a specific intellectual engaged in specific interventions. He was constantly prepared to shift strategies and to question his previous positions. Most of all, he despised dogmatic impositions of theory and the search for universal epistemological or anthropological foundations. It would, of course, be tragically ironic if his discourse were dogmatically imposed on feminism. In the "final" analysis, proof of the value of using Foucault for feminism will be in the puddings, that is, in the practical implications that adopting his methods and insights will have. Attending to the exigencies of feminist practice will sometimes require that we either ignore Foucault or move beyond him. A Foucauldian feminism would require no less.[29]

Notes

Introduction. Disciplining Foucault

1. See "Truth, Power, Self: An Interview With Michel Foucault, October 25, 1982," in *Technologies of the Self,* eds. Luther H. Martin, Huck Gutman and Patrick H. Hutton (Amherst: University of Massachusetts Press, 1988), p. 11.

2. Teresa de Lauretis, "The Technology of Gender," in *Technologies of Gender: Essays on Theory, Film, and Fiction* (Bloomington: University of Indiana Press, 1987), p. 25.

3. Quoted in Carolyn Heilbrun, *Writing a Woman's Life* (New York: Balantine Books), p. 105.

4. I remember being quite depressed as a graduate student upon hearing a paper delivered by a feminist and analytic philosopher inquiring into the possible contributions that philosophy could make to feminism. She concluded that philosophy, as she defined it, could do very little for feminism except perhaps to analyze its arguments since pure philosophical analysis was ideologically neutral. Fortunately, feminists from all philosophical traditions have been able to break away from the definitions of philosophy which produced this type of attitude in the early 1970s. Unfortunately, this conservative view of philosophy is still alive in some quarters.

5. See "Feminism and the Power of Foucauldian Discourse," Chapter 3 in this volume.

6. See, for instance, Jacquelyn Zita, "Historical Amnesia and the Lesbian Continuum," in *Feminist Theory: A Critique of Ideology,* ed. Nannerl Keohane et al. (Chicago: University of Chicago Press, 1982), p. 173.

111

1. Foucault and Feminism

1. See Cherrie Moraga and Gloria Anzaldua, eds. *This Bridge Called My Back: Writings of Radical Women of Color* (Boston: Persephone Press, 1981); Bonnie Thornton Dill, "Race, Class, and Gender: Prospects for an All Inclusive Sisterhood," *Feminist Studies*, Vol. 9, No.1 (1983), pp. 131–50; Floya Anthias and Nira Yuval-Davis, "Contextualizing Feminism—Gender, Ethnic, and Class Divisions," *Feminist Studies*, Vol. 15 (1983), pp. 62–74.

2. Audre Lorde, *Sister Outsider* (New York: Crossing Press, 1984).

3. Ibid., p. 120.

4. Ibid., p. 115.

5. "Revolutionary" feminisms are those which appeal to the notion of a "subject of history" and to the category of a "social totality" in their analyses of the theory and practice of social transformation.

6. Socialist feminism is an obvious alternative to the ones that I have chosen. It represents a theoretical development in feminism which is closest to embodying the basic insights of a politics of difference. See, for example, the work of Linda Nicholson, *Gender and History: The Limits of Social Theory in the Age of the Family* (New York: Columbia University Press, 1986).

7. Meaghan Morris and Paul Patton, eds. *The Pirate's Fiancee: Michel Foucault: Power, Truth, and Strategy* (Sydney: Feral, 1979); and Biddy Martin, "Feminism, Criticism and Foucault," *New German Critique*, Vol. 27, (1982), pp. 3–30.

8. Michel Foucault, Introduction to *Herculin Barbin: Being the Recently Discovered Memoirs of a Nineteenth Century French Hermaphrodite* (New York: Pantheon, 1980), p. 122.

9. Ibid., p. 99.

10. One feminist critic charges that Foucault's institutionalist theory of sexuality results in a picture of the "one-dimensional" containment of sexuality by objective forces beyond our control. She claims that it obscures the "continuous struggles of women against . . . patriarchy." Yet her criticism begs the question since it assumes that an emancipatory theory must rest on the notion of a continuous revolutionary subject. Foucault, after all, is attempting to displace the problem of the subject altogether. See Jacqueline Zita, "Historical Amnesia and the Lesbian Continuum," in *Feminist Theory: A Critique of Ideology*, ed. Nannerl Keohane et al. (Chicago: Chicago University Press, 1982), p. 173.

11. See Foucault's reproduction of the memoirs of a hermaphrodite for an example of his effort to resurrect a knowledge of resistance. This memoir is an account of the despair experienced by Herculine (formerly Alexina) once a

male sexual identity is imposed upon her in her "happy limbo of non-identity." This occurs at a time when the legal and medical profession has become interested in the question of sexual identity and has decided that every individual must be either male or female. Foucault, *Herculin Barbarin*.

12. Michel Foucault, *The History of Sexuality*, Vol. 1: An Introduction, trans. Robert Hurley (New York: Pantheon, 1978), p. 95.

13. Michel Foucault, "The History of Sexuality: An Interview," trans. Geoff Bennington, *Oxford Literary Review*, Vol. 4, No. 2 (1980), p. 13.

14. Michel Foucault, "The Subject and Power," Afterword in Hubert Dreyfus and Paul Rabinow, *Michel Foucault: Beyond Structuralism and Hermeneutics* (Chicago: University of Chicago Press, 1982), p. 221.

15. Ibid., p. 224.

16. Foucault, *Herculin Barbarin*, p. 208.

17. Ibid., p. 82.

18. Ibid., emphasis added.

19. For a similar argument against ahistorical criteria of effective resistance, see Kathryn Pyne Addelson, "Words and Lives," in *Feminist Theory*, ed. Keohane et al., pp. 176–88.

20. John Rajchman, "The Story of Foucault's History," *Social Text*, Vol. 8 (1984), p. 15.

21. Foucault, *Herculin Barbarin*, p. 126.

22. Linda Nicholson describes an explicitly historical feminism in which the search for origins (genealogy) involves an attempt to deconstruct (give an account of the process of construction of) our present categories (e.g., "personal," "public") and thereby free us from a rigid adherence to them. Foucault's genealogies serve the same function. See Nicholson, *Gender and History*.

23. Lorde, *Sister Outsider*, pp. 53–59.

24. Adrienne Rich, "Toward a Woman-centered University," in *On Lies, Secrets and Silence: Selected Prose 1966–1978* (New York: W. W. Norton, 1979), p. 134.

25. Ann Ferguson, "Sex War: The Debate between Radical and Libertarian Feminists," *Signs*, Vol. 10, No. 1, (1984), pp. 106–12.

26. Ibid., p. 110.

27. Rennie Simpson, "The Afro-American Male," in *The Powers of Desire: The Politics of Sexuality*, ed. Ann Snitow, Christine Stansell, and Sharon Thompson (New York: Monthly Review Press, 1983), pp. 229–35.

28. Valerie Amos and Pratibha Parmer, "Challenging Imperial Feminism," *Feminist Review*, Vol. 17 (1984), pp. 1–19.

29. Ann Snitow and Carol Vance, "Towards a Conversation about Sex in Feminism: A Modest Proposal," *Signs*, Vol. 10, No. 1, 1984, p. 132.

30. Ibid., p. 133.

31. Ann Ferguson commented extensively on earlier drafts of this essay and improved it considerably. I also wish to thank Ann Bones of Polity Press for her editorial suggestions.

2. Identity Politics and Sexual Freedom

1. See Alice Echols, "The Taming of the Id: Feminist Sexual Politics," in *Pleasure and Danger: Exploring Female Sexuality,* ed. Carole S. Vance (Boston: Routledge and Kegan Paul, 1984), pp. 50–72. Echols distinguishes "cultural feminism" from early radical feminism and associates the former with the positions here attributed to "radical feminists."

2. See Ann Ferguson's "Sex War: The Debate Between Radical and Libertarian Feminists," *Signs,* vol. 10, No. 1 (1984), pp. 106–12.

3. This is a goal that many radical feminists have affirmed. See *Against Sadomasochism: A Radical Feminist Analysis*, ed. Robin Ruth Linden, D. Pagano, D. Russell, and S. Star. (Palo Alto: Frog in the Well Press, 1982).

4. Ferguson, "Sex War," p. 108.

5. *Ibid.,* p. 109.

6. See, for example, Allison Jaggar, *Feminist Politics and Human Nature* (Totowa, NJ: Rowman and Allenfield, 1983), pp. 106ff.

7. See, for example, Adrienne Rich, *Of Woman Born* (New York: Norton, 1976); Susan Griffin, *Woman and Nature: The Roaring Inside Her* (New York: Harper and Row, 1978). Note some radicals (e.g., Andrea Dworkin) are explicitly opposed to biological determinism.

8. Pat Califia has referred to sexual desire as "impeccably honest." ("Among Us, Against Us—The New Puritans," *The Advocate* (April 17, 1980), p. 14.) Curiously enough, one radical feminist has accused libertarians of appealing to the biological superiority of the female. See Sally Roesch Wagner, "Pornography and the Sexual Revolution: The Backlash of Sadomasochism," in *Against Sadomasochism,* pp. 34ff.

9. On the "dialectical" relationship between biology and culture, see Allison Jaggar, "Human Biology in Feminist Theory: Sexual Equality Reconsidered," in *Beyond Domination* ed. Carol C. Gould (New Jersey: Rowman and Allenheld, 1984), pp. 21–42.

10. See for example Robert Padgug, "Sexual Matters: On Conceptualizing Sexuality in History," *The Radical History Review,* Vol. 20 (Spring/Summer 1979), pp. 3–24; Bert Hansen, "The Historical Construction of Homosexuality," *The*

Radical History Review, Vol. 20 (Spring/Summer, 1979), pp. 66–75; Jeffrey Weeks, *Coming Out: Homosexual Politics in Britain from the Nineteenth Century to the Present* (London: Quartet Books, 1977); Michel Foucault, *The History of Sexuality, Vol. 1, An Introduction,* trans. Robert Hurley (New York: Pantheon, 1978).

11. For examples, see the essays by Sally Roesch Wagner, and Karen Rian in *Against Sadomasochism.* See also Gayle Rubin, "Thinking Sex: Notes for a Radical Theory of the Politics of Sexuality" in *Pleasure and Danger: Exploring Female Sexuality,* pp. 267–319.

12. Sandra Lee Bartky, "Feminine Masochism and the Politics of Personal Transformations," *Hypatia,* Vol. 7, No. 5, pp. 323–34.

13. Rian, *Against Sadomasochism,* pp. 45–50, esp. p. 49. Emphasis mine.

14. Iris Young provides an interesting analysis of the detemporalization of change in her provocative paper "The Ideal of Community and the Politics of Difference," *Social Theory and Practice,* Vol. 12, No. 5 (Spring 1986), pp. 1–26, esp. p. 17.

15. Rubin, "Thinking Sex," p. 277.

16. Michel Foucault, *Power/Knowledge: Selected Interviews and Other Writings, 1972–1977,* ed. Colin Gordon (New York: Pantheon Books, 1980), pp. 219–20.

17. *Ibid.,* p. 220.

18. Ann Ferguson, "Public Patriarchy and How to Fight It: A Tri-Systems Theory," unpublished manuscript.

19. See Ferguson, "Public Patriarchy" for an extended discussion of coalition politics.

20. See John Rajchman, "Ethics after Foucault," *Social Text* (Spring 1986), pp. 165–83, esp. p. 167, for a similar discussion of Foucault's notion of freedom.

21. Rubin, "Thinking Sex," p. 277.

22. *Ibid.,* p. 277.

23. See Chapter 2.

24. Cf. Ernesto Laclau and Chantal Mouffe, *Hegemony and Socialist Strategy: Towards a Radical Democratic Politics,* trans. Winston Moore and Paul Cammack (London: Verso Press, 1985), pp. 188 ff.

25. See Richard Sennett, "Destructive Gemeinschaft," in *The Philosophy of Sex and Love,* ed. Alan Soble (New Jersey: Rowman and Littlefield, 1980), pp. 291–321.

26. *Ibid.,* p. 311.

27. *Ibid.,* p. 312.

28. See Gayle Rubin, "The Traffic in Women: Notes on the 'Political Economy' of

Sex," in *Toward an Anthropology of Women,* ed. Rayna R. Reiter (New York: Monthly Review Press, 1975), pp. 157–210.

29. I owe this phrase to Vicky Spelman.

30. Michel Foucault, "The Subject and Power," afterword in Hubert Dreyfus and Paul Rabinow, *Michel Foucault: Beyond Structuralism and Hermeneutics* (Chicago: University of Chicago Press, 1983), p. 232.

31. Earlier versions of this paper were read at meetings of the Radical Philosophy Association and the National Women's Studies Association. Thanks go to audiences at those meetings and to the following individuals for their comments and suggestions concerning ideas in the essay: Iris Young, Lee Quinby, Irene Diamond and Ann Ferguson.

3. Feminism and the Power of Foucauldian Discourse

1. See, for example, Barbara Ehrenreich and Deirdre English, *For Her Own Good: 150 Years of the Experts' Advise to Women* (New York: Anchor Press, 1978).

2. Sandra Bartky, "Foucault, Femininity and the Modernization of Patriarchal Power" (Paper read at the American Philosophical Association, May 1986), p. 4.

3. See, Chapter 1 and 2. See also Meaghan Morris, "The Pirate's Fiancee," in *Michel Foucault: Power, Truth, and Strategy,* eds. Meaghan Morris and Paul Patton (Sydney: Feral Publications, 1979); Biddy Martin, "Feminism, Criticism and Foucault," *New German Critique,* Vol. 27 (1982), pp. 3–30; Judith Butler, "Variations on Sex and Gender: Beauvoir, Wittig, and Foucault," *Praxis International,* Vol. 5, No. 4 (January 1986), pp. 505–16; Nancy Fraser and Linda Nicholson, "Social Criticism Without Philosophy: An Encounter Between Feminism and Postmodernism," (Paper read at the American Philosophical Association, December 1986), Ruth Bleir, *Science and Gender: A Critique of Biology and Its Theories on Women* (New York: Pergamon Press, 1984); Teresa De Lauretis, *Alice Doesn't: Feminism, Semiotics, Cinema* (Indiana: Indiana University Press, 1984); Donna Haraway, "A Manifesto For Cyborgs: Science, Technology, and Socialist Feminism in the 1980s," *Socialist Review,* Vol. 80 (1985), pp. 65–107.

4. Isaac D. Balbus, "Disciplining Women: Michel Foucault and the Power of Feminist Discourse," in *After Foucault: Humanistic Knowledge, Postmodern Challenges,* ed. Jonathan Arac (New Brunswick: Rutgers University Press 1988), pp. 138–160.

5. Michel Foucault, "Two Lectures," in *Power/Knowledge: Selected Interviews and Other Writings, 1972–1977,* ed. Colin Gordon (New York: Pantheon Press, 1980), p. 83.

6. "Questions of Method: An Interview with Michel Foucault," in *After Philosophy: End or Transformation?* eds. Kenneth Baynes, James Bohman, and Thomas McCarthy (Cambridge: MIT Press, 1987), p. 108.

7. Cf. David Couzens Hoy, "Power, Repression, Progress," in *Foucault: A Critical Reader,* ed. David Couzens Hoy (London: Basil Blackwell, 1986), p. 129.

8. David Hiley, "Foucault and the Analysis of Power: Political Engagement Without Liberal Hope or Comfort," *Praxis International,* Vol. 4, No. 2 (July 1984), pp. 198–99.

9. *Ibid.,* p. 199.

10. Michel Foucault, "Body Power," in *Power/Knowledge,* pp. 60–61.

11. Foucault, "Two Lectures," pp. 80–81.

12. Michel Foucault, "The Subject and Power," afterword to Hubert Dreyfus and Paul Rabinow, *Michel Foucault: Beyond Structuralism and Hermeneutics* (Chicago: University of Chicago Press, 1983), p. 232.

13. Foucault, "Questions of Method," pp. 111–12.

14. Stephen David Ross, "Foucault's Radical Politics," *Praxis International,* Vol. 5, No. 2 (July 1985), p. 134.

15. Michel Foucault, *Herculine Barbin, Being the Recently Discovered Memoirs of a Nineteenth Century Hermaphrodite,* trans. Richard McDougall (New York: Pantheon, 1980).

16. Butler, "Variations on Sex and Gender," p. 515.

17. Michel Foucault, *The History of Sexuality, Vol. 1: An Introduction,* trans. Robert Hurley (New York: Pantheon Press, 1978), p. 95.

18. Foucault, "Two Lectures," p. 81.

19. Foucault, "Questions of Method," p. 110.

20. Balbus, "Disciplining Women," p. 142.

21. *Ibid.,* p. 144.

22. *Ibid.,* p. 148.

23. Jean Grimshaw, *Philosophy and Feminist Thinking,* (Minneapolis: University of Minnesota Press, 1986), p. 63.

24. Bleir, *Science and Gender,* p. 140.

25. *Ibid.,* p. 146.

26. Balbus, "Disciplining Women," p. 160.

27. Butler, "Variations on Sex and Gender," pp. 514–16.

28. Marilyn Frye argues that sexual dimorphism is a culturally enforced phenomenon which constitutes one of the necessary conditions for sexism. She suggests that there is a continuum, not a rigid dichotomy, in the expression of secondary

sex characteristics at the anatomical level. Hence, she too could envision the possibility of more than two genders. See Marilyn Frye, "Sexism," in *The Politics of Reality: Essays in Feminist Theory* (New York: Crossing Press, 1983), pp. 17–40.

29. Fraser and Nicholson, "Social Criticism Without Philosophy," pp. 20–21.

30. Ian Hacking, "The Archaeology of Foucault," in *Foucault: A Critical Reader*, p. 39.

31. Audre Lorde, *Sister Outsider* (New York: Crossing Press, 1984), p. 120.

32. I want to thank Jonathan Arac for his comments on an earlier draft of this paper.

4. Disciplining Mothers

1. See Michel Foucault, *The History of Sexuality, Vol. 1: An Introduction*, trans. Robert Hurley (New York: Pantheon, 1978), pp. 140ff.

2. Ibid., p. 141.

3. See the following: Rita Arditti, Renate Duelli-Klein and Shelley Minden, *Test-Tube Women: What Future For Motherhood?* (Boston: Pandora Press, 1984); Gena Corea, *The Mother Machine: Reproductive Technologies from Artificial Insemination to Artificial Wombs* (New York: Harper & Row, 1985); Mary Daly, *Gyn/Ecology* (Boston: Beacon Press, 1978); Barbara Ehrenreich and Deirdre English, *For Her Own Good: 150 Years of Expert's Advice to Women* (London: Pluto Press, 1979); Linda Gordon, *Woman's Body, Woman's Right: A Social History of Birth Control in America* (New York: Penguin Books, 1977); Ruth Hubbard, *The Politics of Women's Biology* (New Brunswick: Rutgers University Press, 1990); Rosalind Petchesky, *Abortion and Woman's Choice* (New York: Longman Press, 1984); Adrienne Rich, *Of Woman Born: Motherhood as Experience and Institution* (New York: W.W. Norton, 1976).

4. See Gena Corea, *The Mother Machine*.

5. For other critiques of the new reproductive technologies which share Corea's approach, see the anthology edited by Patricia Spallone and Deborah Lynn Steinberg, *Made to Order: The Myth of Reproductive and Genetic Progress* (Oxford: Pergamon Press, 1987); also see Corea, et al. *Man-Made Woman: How the New Reproductive Technologies Affect Women* (Bloomington: Indiana University Press 1987). The positions of Corea and other radical feminists have been critically assessed by many of the authors writing in Michelle Stanworth's anthology, *Reproductive Technologies: Gender, Motherhood and Medicine*, (Minneapolis: University of Minnesota Press, 1987).

6. Jana Sawicki, "Heidegger and Foucault on Technological Nihilism," *Philosophy and Social Criticism*, Vol. 13, No. 2 (1987), pp. 155–173.

7. See, for example, Teresa de Lauretis, *Technologies of Gender* (Bloomington: Indiana University Press, 1987); and "Eccentric Subjects: Feminist Theory and Historical Consciousness," *Feminist Studies*, Vol. 16, No.1 (Spring 1990), pp. 115–150.

8. See, for example, Shelley Minden, "Patriarchal Designs: The Genetic Engineering of Human Embryos," in *Made to Order,* and Ruth Hubbard, *The Politics of Women's Biology.*

9. By "technology" I am referring not simply to the instruments but to the procedures and rules which govern their use, a set of techniques, and, more generally, a way of looking at things and processes which objectifies them for the purpose of controlling them. I do not regard technologies as inherently dominating. Control and domination are not equivalent. Thus, I assume that in every society some type of technology is both desirable and inevitable.

10. See Keller, "Baconian Science: The Arts of Mastery and Obedience," in *Reflections on Science and Gender* (New Haven: Yale University Press, 1985), pp. 33–42.

11. Ibid., p. 36.

12. Ibid., p. 42.

13. I am not suggesting that radical feminists adhere to this psychoanalytic account, but rather that the account provides one type of theoretical support for their claims that men have a primordial desire to procreate.

14. See Nancy Schrom Dye, "History of Childbirth in America," *Signs*, Vol. 6, No. 1 (1980), pp. 97–108 for a balanced feminist historiographical essay on the history of childbirth. See also Deborah A. Sullivan and Rose Weitz, *Labor Pains: Modern Midwives and Homebirths* (New Haven: Yale University Press, 1988), for a feminist history of midwifery. For more provocative and radical feminist histories of the medicalization of women's bodies and the history of midwifery, see Barbara Ehrenreich and Deirdre English, *Witches, Midwives and Nurses: A History of Women Healers* (Trumansburg, NY: Feminist Press, 1973), and by the same authors, *For Her Own Good: 150 Years of Experts' Advice to Women*. See also, Gena Corea, *The Hidden Malpractice* (New York: Harper and Row, 1985).

15. The term "medicalization" usually implies the negative phenomenon of reducing political, personal and social issues to medical problems thereby giving scientific experts the power to "solve" them within the constraints of medical practice. I will retain this negative definition throughout this paper. However, I do believe that pregnancy, childbirth and infertility are healthcare issues and should continue to be treated as such. Of course, I do not think that medical professionals should monopolize authority over all issues raised in this context.

16. Jalna Hamner, "Transforming Consciousness: Women and the New Reproduc-

tive Technologies," in *Man-Made Women*, p. 94. See also, in the same volume, Robyn Rowland, "Motherhood, Patriarchal Power, Alienation and the Issue of 'Choice' in Sex Preselection," pp. 74–87.

17. See "Resolution from the FINRRAGE Conference, July 3–8, 1985, Vallinge, Sweden," in *Made to Order*, pp. 211–12.

18. See Corea, *The Mother Machine*, p. 319.

19. See Carolyn Merchant, *The Death of Nature: Women, Ecology and the Scientific Revolution* (New York: Harper and Row 1980).

20. Quoted in Jurgen Habermas, "Technology and Science as Ideology," in *Toward a Rational Society* (Boston: Beacon Press, 1970), p. 84. In this essay Habermas rejects Marcuse's romantic tendency to treat science and technology as wholly ideological as well as his appeals to a new science and technology. He argues instead for the restoration of democratic forms of legitimation in opposition to the tendency for a technocratic society to repress ethical and political reflection on technological practices and interventions in social processes in favor of merely technological reflection. In other words, he argues for a repoliticization of issues currently being addressed as technical problems and against the view that modern technology is inherently dominating. Despite other differences, I believe that Habermas and Foucault were in agreement about the need to repoliticize "technical" problems.

21. Ibid., pp. 86–87.

22. As Susan Bordo points out in her feminist appropriation of Foucault, denying that the history of women's bodies is the product of patriarchal conspiracies

> does not mean that individuals do not consciously pursue goals that advance their own positions, and advance certain power positions in the process. But it does deny that in doing so they are directing the overall movement of relations, or engineering their shape. They may not ever know what the shape is. Nor does the fact that power relations involve the domination of particular groups—say, prisoners by guards, females by males, amateurs by experts—entail that the dominators are in control of the situation, or that the dominated do not sometimes advance and extend the situation themselves.

See her "Anorexia Nervosa: Psychopathology as the Crystallization of Culture," in *Feminism and Foucault: Reflections on Resistance* eds. Irene Diamond and Lee Quinby (Boston: Northeastern University Press, 1988), p. 91.

23. See especially the work of Teresa de Lauretis cited above.

24. Paula A. Treichler, "Feminism, Medicine and the Meaning of Childbirth," in *Body/Politics: Women and the Discourses of Science,* eds. Mary Jacobus, Evelyn Fox Keller, and Sally Shuttleworth (New York: Routledge, 1990), p. 118.

25. See *Labor Pains*, p. 38.

26. See Susan Bordo's "Anorexia Nervosa" and Sandra Bartky's "Foucault, Femininity and Patriarchal Power," in *Foucault and Feminism* for two examples of analyses of how disciplinary practices produce specifically feminine forms of embodiment through the development of dietary and fitness regimens, pathologies related to them, and expert advice on how to walk, talk, dress, wear makeup, and so forth.

27. Linda Singer, "Bodies, Pleasures, Powers," *differences*, Vol. 1 (Winter 1989), p. 57.

28. Emily Martin, *The Woman in the Body: A Cultural Analysis of Reproduction* (Boston: Beacon Press, 1987), p. 21.

29. For a fascinating account of a specific set of struggles over the interpretation of needs, see Nancy Fraser, "Women, Welfare and the Politics of Needs Interpretation," in *Unruly Practices: Power, Discourse and Gender in Contemporary Social Theory* (Minneapolis: University of Minnesota Press, 1989), pp. 144–60.

30. Michel Foucault, "Two Lectures," in *Power/Knowledge: Selected Interviews and Other Writings, 1972–1977*, ed. Colin Gordon (New York: Pantheon Books, 1980), p. 82.

31. "Reproduction and Gender Hierarchy: Amniocentesis in Contemporary America," paper presented at an International Symposium of the Wenner-Gren Foundation for Anthropological Research, January 10–18, 1987, Mijas, Spain.

32. Ibid., p. 24.

33. See Sandra Lee Bartky, "Foucault, Femininity and the Modernization of Patriarchal Power."

34. Linda Gordon, "The Struggle for Reproductive Freedom: Three Stages of Feminism," in *Capitalist Patriarchy and the Case for Socialist Feminism*, ed. Zillah Eisenstein (New York: Monthly Review Press, 1979), pp. 107–32.

35. See Marge Piercy, *Woman on the Edge of Time* (New York: Knopf, 1976), for a futuristic model of high technology childbirth that embodies feminist principles.

36. Donna Haraway, "A Manifesto for Cyborgs: Science, Technology and Socialist Feminism in the 1980s," *Socialist Review*, Vol. 80 (1985), p. 66.

37. Ibid., p. 72.

38. Treichler, "Feminism, Medicine and the Meaning of Childbirth," p. 131.

39. Earlier versions of this paper were presented to audiences at Vassar College, MIT, Northwestern University, and Notre Dame University. I wish to thank them for their helpful questions and comments. Special thanks go to Iris Young, Linda Singer, Nancy Fraser, Linda Nicholson, Sharon Barker and members of

Sofphia (Socialist Feminist Philosophers) for helpful conversations and comments on previous drafts.

5. Foucault and Feminism: A Critical Reappraisal

1. See essays by Susan Bordo, Sandra Bartky, Judith Butler, Teresa de Lauretis, Nancy Fraser, and Iris Young cited throughout this volume.

2. Of course, the impact of Foucault's work was different in the United States, where even liberals are on the defensive, than it was in France where Marxism still represents a viable theoretical alternative among the intelligentsia and where there is a mass-based socialist party. There is a danger that Foucault's work could serve to bolster already strong opposition to the idea of radical politics in this country. One critical theorist, Martin Jay, has suggested that Foucault's pluralism has conservative implications as a political strategy in the United States, where liberal pluralism is already presumably operating. See his *Marxism and Totality: The Adventures of a Concept from Lukacs to Habermas* (Berkeley: University of California Press, 1985), pp. 513–14, fn. 14. It is, of course, important to challenge assimilations of Foucault's discourse that undermine its radical implications. His "pluralism" is, of course, quite distinct from liberal pluralism. It is more akin to the radical pluralist position developed by Ernesto Laclau and Chantal Mouffe in *Hegemony and Socialist Strategy: Towards a Radical Democratic Politics,* trans. Winston Moore and Paul Cammack (London: Verso Press, 1985).

3. Linda Alcoff, "Feminism and Foucault: The Limits to a Collaboration," in *Crises in Continental Philosophy,* eds. Arlene Dallery and Charles Scott (New York: State University of New York Press, 1990), pp. 69–86.

4. Nancy Fraser argues very convincingly that Foucault seems to offer no systematic normative basis for his political interventions in her article, "Foucault on Modern Power: Empirical Insights and Normative Confusions," *Praxis International,* Vol. 1 (October 1981), pp. 272–87. I agree with Fraser that there is normative confusion in Foucault's critique of modern forms of power/ knowledge, particularly as it is developed in *Discipline and Punish.* Some of this confusion is clarified in later interviews and in *The History of Sexuality* when he suggests that he wrote as an engaged and specific intellectual who was not rejecting modernity *tout court,* but rather using genealogy as a means of challenging specific modern practices and specific uses of liberal and liberationist discourses to mask the effects of domination. Moreover, after the publication of *Discipline and Punish* Foucault attempted to distinguish "power" from "domination." He defines domination as a situation in which a subject is unable to overturn the domination relation, that is, a situation where resistance has

been overcome. In contrast, power relations constantly face resistance and the possibility of a reversal. He states:

> In many cases the relations of power are fixed in such a way that they are perpetually assymmetrical and the margin of liberty is extremely limited. To take an example . . . in the traditional conjugal relation in . . . the eighteenth and nineteenth centuries, we cannot say that there was only male power; the woman herself could do a lot of things: be unfaithful to him, extract money from him, refuse him sexually. She was, however, subject to a state of domination, in the measure where all that was finally no more than a certain number of tricks which never brought about a reversal of the situation. In these cases of domination—economic, social, institutional, or sexual—the problem is in fact to find out where resistance is going to organize.

See "The Ethic of Care for the Self as a Practice of Freedom: An Interview with Michel Foucault on January 20, 1984," in *The Final Foucault*, eds. James Bernauer and David Rasmussen, (Cambridge: MIT Press, 1988), pp. 12–13.

Yet, Foucault is never very clear about what makes domination a malevolent phenomenon. He suggests in the above passage that domination interferes with personal liberty, but most often seems to assume that it is self-evident that domination ought to be resisted. (Presumably, from some point "outside" the specific situation of domination.) My own appropriation of Foucault is one that attempts to bypass some of this normative confusion by presupposing a normative framework that includes concepts such as domination, justice, rights and liberties and regards them as essentially contested concepts. (See especially my "Disciplining Mothers: Feminism and the New Reproductive Technologies" in this volume.)

5. Nancy Hartsock, "Rethinking Modernism: Minority vs. Majority Theories," *Cultural Critique* Vol. 7 (Fall 1987), pp. 187–206; Barbara Christian, "The Race for Theory," *Cultural Critique* Vol. 6 (Spring 1987), pp. 51–63.

6. Foucault says of his own critique:

> A critique is not a matter of saying that things are not right as they are. It is a matter of pointing out on what kinds of assumptions, what kinds of familiar, unchallenged, unconsidered modes of thought the practices we accept rest. . . . Thought exists independently of systems and structures of discourse. It is something that is often hidden, but which always animates everyday behavior. There is always a little thought even in the most stupid institutions; there is always thought even in silent habits. . . . Criticism is a matter of flushing out that thought and trying to change it: to show that things are not as self-evident as one believed, to see that what is accepted as self-evident will no longer be accepted as such. . . . In these circumstances, criticism

(and radical criticism) is absolutely indispensable for any transformation. . . . [A]s soon as one can no longer think things as one formerly thought them, transformation becomes both very urgent, very difficult and quite possible.

See *Michel Foucault: Politics, Philosophy and Culture—Interviews and Other Writings, 1977–1984*, ed. Lawrence D. Kritzman, trans. Alan Sheridan and others, (New York: Routledge, 1988), p. 154.

7. See John Rajchman's excellent study of Foucault, *Michel Foucault: The Freedom of Philosophy* (New York: Columbia University Press, 1985), pp. 29ff. for an analysis of Foucault's position as "homosexual author."

8. David Couzens Hoy develops an argument similar to this one in his introduction to *Foucault: A Critical Reader*, ed. David Couzens Hoy (New York: Basil Blackwell, 1986), pp. 14ff.

9. This is an essentially pragmatic line of thinking which enables us to appeal to contemporary standards of rationality and justice without grounding them in ahistorical foundations. For a similar line of argument see Nancy Fraser, "Foucault's Body Language: A Posthumanist Political Rhetoric?" in *Unruly Practices*, pp. 55–66.

10. Evidence that Foucault does not reject appeals to modern forms of rationality is found in the following statement where he discusses the nature of his objections to Jurgen Habermas's idea of a communicative praxis free of coercive constraints and effects. He speaks of the need for the development of "practices of liberty" or an ethics of the self:

> I don't believe that there can be a society without relations of power, if you understand them as means by which individuals try to conduct, to determine the behavior of others. The problem is not of trying to dissolve them in the utopia of a perfectly transparent communication, but to give one's self the rules of law, the techniques of management, and also the ethics, the **ethos**, the practice of self, which would allow these games of power to be played with a minimum of domination.

See "The Ethic of Care for the Self as a Practice of Freedom," p. 18.

11. Foucault states:

> What we call humanism has been used by Marxists, liberals, Nazis, Catholics. This does not mean that we have to get rid of what we call human rights, but that we can't say that freedom or human rights has to be limited to certain frontiers. . . . What I am afraid of about humanism is that it presents a certain form of our ethics as a universal model for any kind of freedom. I think that there are more secrets, more possible freedoms, and more inventions in our future than we can imagine in humanism as it is dogmatically represented on every side of the political rainbow.

See "Truth, Power, Self: An Interview with Michel Foucault," in *Technologies of the Self,* eds. Luther H. Martin, Huck Gutman and Patrick Hutton (Amherst: The University of Massachusetts Press, 1988), p. 15.

12. In one of his last interviews Foucault commented:

> I do not mean to say that liberation or such and such a form of liberation does not exist. When a colonial people tries to free itself of its colonizer, that is truly an act of liberation, in the strict sense of the word. But as we also know, . . . in this extremely precise example, this act of liberation is not sufficient to establish the practices of liberty that later on will be necessary for this people, this society and these individuals to decide upon receivable and acceptable forms of their existence or political society.

See "The Ethic of Care for the Self as a Practice of Freedom," p. 3.

13. Rajchman, *Michel Foucault: The Freedom of Philosophy,* p. 38.

14. See my "Feminism and the Power of Foucauldian Discourse," in this volume.

15. I use "we" here as both a provocation and an invitation and not with the presumption that it captures the sentiments of all women who identify as feminists. Moreover, as my imperatives indicate, I clearly do not believe that feminists should refrain from making political judgments.

16. See Ann Ferguson, "Sex War: The Debate between Radical and Libertarian Feminists," *Signs, Vol.* 10, No. 1 (1984), pp. 106–12. See also, Ferguson, *Blood at the Root: Motherhood, Sexuality and Male Domination* (London: Pandora Press, 1989).

17. See Chris Weedon, *Feminist Practice and Poststructuralist Theory* (New York: Basil Blackwell, 1987) for a similar account of Foucault's subject.

18. The subject presupposed in Foucault's later discourses resembles the creative, nihilating subject found in the writings of French existentialist, Jean-Paul Sartre.

19. Alison Jaggar and Rachel Martin develop the outlines of an alternative model of consciousness-raising in "Literacy: New Words for a New World," paper delivered at Sofphia, October 1988, Mt. Holyoke College.

20. Sandra Bartky, "Toward a Phenomenology of Feminist Consciousness," *Feminism and Philosophy,* eds. Mary Vetterling-Braggin, Frederick Elliston and Jane English (Totowa, NJ: Littlefield, Adams and Co., 1981), pp. 22–34.

21. See Caren Kaplan, "Deterritorialization: The Rewriting of Home and Exile in Western Feminist Discourse," *Cultural Critique,* Vol. 6 (Spring 1987), p. 191.

22. Christian, "The Race for Theory," pp. 57ff.

23. In her book *Gender Trouble,* Judith Butler develops a powerful argument against the idea that feminist theorists need to develop a unified account of feminine identity as a common ground for feminist politics. She endorses

Foucault's descriptions of modern sexual identities as principle targets of dominating regulatory mechanisms and offers a radical critique of the political construction of identity. When I speak of the dangers of Foucault's strategy of self-refusal for feminism, and of its dangers for women who have little sense of self to refuse, I am not suggesting that the remedy is to build a unified feminist subject, but rather to develop the sense of self-esteem, confidence and autonomy necessary for actively resisting the domination associated with former identities that were often assumed unconsciously. Presumably, building this sort of self is not only compatible with a radical inquiry into the political regulation of identity, but also necessary for it. In other words, I am not claiming that feminism requires any essentialist view of feminine identity to underpin its politics, but rather that feminist politics requires agents who are capable of self-assertion and self-esteem. In effect, I am arguing against a possible effect of Foucault's strategy of self-refusal, namely the further disempowerment of oppressed groups. See *Gender Trouble: Feminism and the Subversion of Identity* (New York: Routledge, 1990).

24. Adrienne Rich, "Resisting Amnesia: History and Personal Life," *Blood, Bread, and Poetry: Selected Prose, 1979–1985* (New York: W.W. Norton, 1986), p. 144.

25. Teresa de Lauretis, "Eccentric Subjects: Feminist Theory and Historical Consciousness," *Feminist Studies*, Vol. 16, No. 1 (Spring 1990), p. 138.

26. Ibid., p. 138–9.

27. Ibid., p. 138.

28. Ibid., p. 126.

29. I wish to thank Iris Young, Josephine Donovan, Sandra Bartky, Linda Nicholson, Michael Howard, Roger King and Tony Brinkley for their helpful comments on earlier drafts of this paper.

Index